God of Our Fathers?

About the Author

Peter Vardy was a practising chartered accountant and public company chairman before becoming, at the age of 39, lecturer in Philosophy of Religion at Heythrop College, University of London. He has a Masters degree in theology and doctorate from Kings College London and also runs the Philosophy of Religion component of the Masters degree course at London University's Institute of Education. He is a committed Anglican and is married with five children.

David L. Edwards, Provost of Southwark Cathedral, writes about *God of Our Fathers?*:

'The reduction of traditional Christianity into a belief in the God who inspires rather than acts, or suffers rather than controls, or its further reduction into the practice of self-purifying meditation, has often been proposed as a solution to its problems in a West which is heavily secularised. Here the pros and cons of this policy are set out lucidly by a theologian who is still sufficiently in touch with his own background as a businessman to know that these great questions deserve something more than slogans or jargon.'

John McDade sj (Editor of 'The Month') writes:

'We badly need a clear guide to the important philosophical questions about the truth of religious belief—this book is exceptional in the clarity and simplicity with which these questions are discussed. Peter Vardy is an excellent teacher! The book is accessible and masterly in the way that the author presents the range of possible approaches to central questions. Highly recommended.'

GOD OF OUR FATHERS?

Do We Know What We Believe?

PETER VARDY

Darton, Longman and Todd
London

First published in 1987 by
Darton, Longman and Todd Ltd
89 Lillie Road, London SW6 1UD

© 1987 Peter Vardy

ISBN 0 232 51716 9

British Library Cataloguing in Publication Data

Vardy, Peter
    God of our fathers?: do we know what we believe?
    1. God
    I. Title
    291.2′11   BL205

    ISBN 0–232–51716–9

Phototypeset by Input Typesetting Ltd, London SW19 8DR
Printed and bound in Great Britain by
Anchor Brendon Ltd, Tiptree, Essex

To my wife, Anne
With thanks for encouragement, patience, tolerance, love –
and five children!
AMOR VINCIT OMNIA

Contents

CONTENTS

Acknowledgements

The Scripture quotations in this book are from the Revised Standard Version of the Bible, copyrighted 1971 and 1952 by the Division of Christian Education of the National Council of Churches of Christ in the USA.

My thanks are due to present and past students at Heythrop and Kings Colleges and Masters degree students at the Institute of Education (University of London) for many enjoyable and helpful discussions on the matters dealt with in this book.

PETER VARDY
St Clair, Devon,
and Heythrop College, London

Easter/Pentecost 1986

1

A Defiled and Mutilated Word

The Jewish writer and theologian, Martin Buber, was staying on a great German estate in 1932 and had got up early to read the proofs of a book. He met a 'noble old thinker' as Buber described him, already up before him, and at this thinker's request read the proofs aloud. When Buber was finished, the old man said with great vehemence:

How can you bring yourself to say 'God' time after time? How can you expect your readers will take the word in the sense that you wish it to be taken? What you mean by the name God is something beyond all human grasp and comprehension, but in speaking about it you have lowered it to human conceptualisation. What word of all human speech is so misused, so defiled, so desecrated as this! All the innocent blood that has been shed for it has robbed it of its radiance. All the injustice that it has been used to cover has effaced its features. When I hear 'God' it sometimes seems blasphemous.*

Buber says he sat, silent. Then he felt as if a power from on high entered into him and what he then replied he says that he can only indicate. It was as follows:

Yes, it is the most heavy-laden of all human words. None has become so soiled, so mutilated. Just for this reason I may not abandon it. Generations of men have laid the

* The quotations from Buber are translated by Bernhard Schonemann, a student at Kings College, London (1983–86), from Buber's 'Gottesfinsternis: Betrachtungen zur Beziehung zwischen Religion und Philosophie', in *Werke Bd. I: Schriften zur Philosophie* (Munchen – Heidelberg 1962), pp. 508–10).

1

burden of their anxious lives upon this word and weighed it to the ground: it lies in the dust and bears their whole burden. The races of men with their religious factions have torn the word to pieces; they have killed for it and died for it, and it bears their finger-marks and their blood. Where might I find a word like it to describe the highest? If I took the purest, most sparkling concept from the treasure chambers of the philosophers, I could only capture thereby an unbinding product of thought. I could not capture the presence of Him whom the generations of men have honoured and degraded with their awesome living and dying. I do indeed mean Him whom the hell-tormented and heaven-storming generations of men mean. Certainly they draw caricatures and write 'God' underneath; they murder one another and say in 'God's' name. But when all madness and delusion fall to dust, when they stand over against Him in the loneliest darkness and no longer say 'He, He' but rather sigh 'Thou', shout 'Thou', all of them with one word, and when they then add 'God', is it not the real God whom they implore, the One living God, the God of the children of man? Is it not He who *hears* them? And just for this reason, is not the word 'God' the word of appeal, a word which has become a *name*, consecrated in all tongues for all times? We must esteem those who interdict it because they rebel against the injustice and wrong which are so readily referred to 'God' for authorisation. But we may not give it up. How understandable it is that some should suggest that we should remain silent about the 'last things' for a time in order that the misused words may be redeemed! But they are not to be redeemed *thus*. We cannot cleanse the word God and we cannot make it whole; but, defiled and mutilated as it is, we can raise it from the ground and set it over an hour of great care.

The old man got up, came over to Buber and laid his hand on his shoulder and said, 'Come, let us be friends.'

This book explores different conceptions of God that are found among theologians and philosophers today and examines their implications for religion – including talk of miracles, prayer, life after death, eternal life and evil. It does not attempt to raise the defiled word 'God' from the ground onto some new pinnacle, but rather to examine soberly and clearly the implications of different approaches to 'God', so that believers and others can decide for themselves where they stand in relation to the word and the consequences of the views they hold.

2

Background

1 Introduction

Love exists, so does the wind and so do chairs. Believers hold that God exists – but what does this mean?

What is God? God has been at the heart of most human endeavours and yet few words are so poorly defined. What is even more surprising is that most people think they know what the word means.

In this book we shall be looking at a number of different meanings of God and discussing their significance. All the meanings are plausible and are held, in one form or another, by eminent theologians and philosophers as well as by ordinary people. However the significance of the different meanings are often not understood. Thus a distinguished professor or bishop may appear on television or radio talking about religion and the religious attitude to life, but almost everything he says is going to be based on the idea of God with which he is operating. He (or she) will, however, rarely tell listeners clearly about his or her position and, therefore, it is not always easy for the listener to fully understand the approach that is being taken.

In a recent opinion poll in Britain, 80 per cent of those interviewed said that they believed in God. They were not questioned further, but their ideas would probably have been found to be very vague. The idea of God is part of the education process, yet it is often surrounded by mystery as well as words used by Church 'professionals' that are not always easy to understand. The result is that it can be somewhat difficult for even the intelligent and interested layman to understand just what is being said. In this book the number of technical terms will be kept to a minimum and, where they are used, they will be defined. If you are in doubt as to the meaning of a word, refer to the index at the back of the book which will give you the page reference where it is defined.

This book is intended as an introduction which, I hope, will lead to further reading. This inevitably means that there is always much more that could be said in every area. References are kept to an absolute minimum, but at the end of the book there are suggestions for further reading in different areas.

2 Sources of ideas

(a) Plato and the Forms. There are four basic approaches that can be taken to the meaning of God. Before considering these it is necessary to look briefly at the philosophy of Plato as his views had a great influence on those who came after him and on the way in which the Church formulated some of its ideas of God.

Plato's God was called the Demiurge. The Demiurge made the world out of material which already existed (i.e. he did not create it). This material was chaotic and without any order at all. Just like a potter makes a pot using material which he did not create, so the Demiurge fashioned the universe. However he had a model to work from and this model, Plato thought, was the 'Forms'.

The Platonic idea of the Forms is complicated and a simple outline is all that is necessary here. On earth we are familiar with goodness, beauty, truth, justice and similar ideas. However the instances we see of these are obviously not perfect instances. We know people who are good, but that does not mean they are perfect; we know others who are beautiful, truthful or just, but we do not know perfect examples of these. Plato considered that if someone or something is good, beautiful, just and the like they in some way participate or share in the perfect Form of Goodness, Beauty, Truth or Justice (notice that a capital letter is used when referring to a Form whereas a small letter is used when referring to examples that resemble this form – thus examples of justice participate in and thus partly resemble the perfect Form of

Justice). These pefect Forms are real and they exist; they are immaterial entities.

Plato maintained that anything that is truly perfect must be completely unchangeable. If something could change then either it would be getting better or it would be getting worse and in neither case could it be perfect. The Forms, therefore, as they represented perfect Goodness, Beauty, Truth, Justice, etc. would also have to be completely unchangeable – they would be IMMUTABLE (unchanging), TIMELESS (outside time so that time did not pass for them) and SPACELESS (outside space – you could not, therefore, visit one of the Platonic Forms in a spaceship however far you travelled!)

Plato's Demiurge used these timeless and spaceless Forms as a model to fashion the universe out of the pre-existent material that was available. However the universe necessarily had to be an imperfect model because the universe is in time and space whilst the Forms were not. The Demiurge, therefore, did as good a job as he could with the material that he had available. In a similar way the sculptor who wishes to produce a casting of 'the wind' would have to produce as good a work of art as he could using the materials he has to work from and recognising that he is casting in bronze something which you cannot see and which moves whilst the bronze can be seen and does not move. The finished sculpture may capture something of the flavour and power of the wind, but it cannot be an altogether accurate picture.

(b) The biblical approach. In the Old Testament, God walks in the garden with Adam, he appears to Moses in the burning bush, he wrestles with Jacob, and he changes his mind (for instance, in Genesis 18 when Abraham persuades God to alter his plans for the destruction of Sodom if there are first fifty, then forty-five, then forty, then thirty, then twenty and finally just ten just men in the city. Again, in Genesis 19, Lot persuades God to let him flee to a nearby 'little city' and not to 'the hills', and there are many other examples). God talks to the prophets and has favourites on no very clear grounds (starting with the 'chosen people' of Israel, who were not selected from all the other peoples in the world because they were the most loyal or the most moral). In short, the God that appears through the pages of the Old Testament is

ANTHROPOMORPHIC; in other words he is visualised as being in many respects like man. Indeed Genesis records that God says: 'Let us make man in our image, after our likeness' (1:26).

This idea that man is made in the image of God is found throughout the Bible. Of course, the biblical writers constantly point out that God is much more than just a 'super-man' – heaven itself cannot contain him. In part, they were reacting against any idea of God conceived as a graven image. Their God was not an idol, able to be fashioned by man, but an individual who could create, who could act and who was closely involved with the world. What is more, God is OMNIPRESENT (he is constantly present everywhere), and the Psalmist says:

> If I ascend to heaven, thou art there! . . .
> If I take the wings of the morning
>   and dwell in the uttermost parts of the sea,
> even there thy hand shall lead me
>   and thy right hand shall hold me. (Ps. 139:8–10)

And wilt God indeed walk upon the earth? Behold Heaven and the highest Heaven cannot contain thee. (1 Kings 8:27)

God is seen in the Old Testament as gradually revealing himself to his chosen people, but what is revealed is a God they can at least to some extent understand. God is seen to be both anthropomorphic and yet as being above anything that the writers of the Old Testament can imagine. Constantly these writers refuse to limit God, they refuse to put him in a 'box' so that he can be analysed. However, God clearly appears (at least on a straightforward reading) as an individual who is tremendously concerned with everything that happens in the world. The biblical God is also unlike Plato's Demiurge in that he creates the universe 'EX NIHILO' (literally from nothing – God 'utters' the world into existence; he says 'Let there be light' (Gen. 1:3) and there is light). In other words the biblical God is not limited by having to use pre-existent material nor does he have to rely on any Platonic 'Forms' for a model.

The biblical writers do not give any clear impression of

heaven, but they consider it to be a social kingdom where there are both good and bad beings who interact with each other. It is a kingdom of peace and tranquility, as Isaiah says: 'The wolf shall dwell with the lamb, and the leopard shall lie down with the kid; and the calf and the young lion and the fatling together, and a little child shall lead them' (Isa. 11:6). These themes are continued in the New Testament. Jesus speaks of God as 'Father', and the picture of heaven that he gives is again of a heavenly society made up of individuals full of the praise and glory of God.

Having said this, however, the biblical picture clearly requires interpretation. The Bible is not to be taken altogether literally. As an example, the Old Testament uses pictures of God which may best be described as helpful ways for believers to think about God rather than literal statements. Relatively few believers, for instance, take the Genesis story literally (although a small minority certainly do so). Through this story, the biblical writers portrayed the dependence of the world on God. The literal meaning of the story is unclear and is much debated. If, therefore, the Bible needs to be interpreted, much is going to depend on: (i) the perspective from which this interpretation takes place; and (ii) the extent to which the Bible can be seen as making literal statements about God and his activity in the world.

These are vital questions to which the Bible itself is not going to provide the answer. It is necessary to go beyond the biblical material itself to decide how the Bible is to be understood. We shall see in the next chapter that there is a major divide between those who feel that much of the Bible is to be taken literally when it talks about God and those who consider that it speaks to the believer by way of metaphor.

(c) The early Church. The writers of the early Church had, therefore, at least two major influences affecting them. On the one hand they had the whole of the Jewish, Hebrew tradition which saw God on anthropomorphic lines and on the other hand they had the influence of Greek philosophy. The influence of the Greeks varied between the different Fathers – St Augustine, for one, was strongly influenced by Plato although for others the influence was considerably less.

8

It must be remembered that the Fathers of the early Church were largely living and writing within the Roman Empire. The Romans did not themselves have many philosophers considering questions about God and his relationship to the universe – although they tended to respect the ancient Greek figures (to the extent that they were aware of them). The Church Fathers, therefore, tried to bring these two views together, and produced a combination which has never been wholly satisfactory. The two views *are* different and, whilst they can be forced together, they form an uneasy alliance. In our discussions of God, much is going to depend on whether the Greek (meaning the Platonic) or the straightforwardly biblical view is given supremacy and which view is used to interpret the other.

It is easy to see that, if you have accepted Plato's idea that the truly perfect must be the completely unchanging, then God (who is by definition perfect) must be timeless and spaceless and wholly immutable. If he is not, then he could not (in Plato's view) be perfect. Further, if God is outside time and space, he can be thought of as the creator of both of them. If, however, God is *within* time and space, then he might be considered to be limited by time and space. The more these options were considered, the clearer the position seemed. God must, many of the early Church Fathers felt, be timeless and spaceless, as all time could then be equally present to him. He could, therefore, be OMNISCIENT (he could know everything in the past, present and future absolutely). This was considered to be vital, as only if God knew the future in detail could the believer be sure that all would turn out in accordance with the divine plan.

A timeless and spaceless God could see everyone at all points on the road of time. Thus the creation of the universe, Caesar's invasion of Britain and whatever prayers you may say on your deathbed will all be *simultaneously* present to God. We thus have the picture of a timeless, spaceless, immutable God who is OMNIPOTENT (he can do anything – although we shall have to consider in due course just what this means), omnipresent and omniscient. It was an attractive picture and was accepted by much of the Christian Church for more than one thousand four hundred years. It has, however, very considerable problems.

We must now turn to consider the available alternative meanings of God.

3

What is God?

This chapter will not aim to solve the problem of what God is. This is much too complex, and almost all religious writers would want to say that God is other than man and cannot be fully understood or comprehended. Instead four possible views of God will be given. They have been kept as simple as possible and, therefore, do not include the sophisticated features that many of their academic advocates may consider desirable. They should, however, be easily understood, and I shall be referring constantly to these four conceptions as this book progresses. When the meaning of miracle, prayer, evil, the existence of God, eternal life and similar issues are discussed, the view that is taken of God is going to have a decisive influence.

Each of the four options will be discussed under a simple heading. In all cases, the term used as a heading should be regarded as verbal shorthand. Thus the first option is referred to as 'God as personal and everlasting', and I hope the meaning of this will be clear from the discussion below. The heading terms have been chosen as they reflect the flavour of the view without representing an adequate description. This chapter is, therefore, particularly important in order that the significance of each of the four heading terms can be understood.

1 God as personal and everlasting

In the previous chapter the origins of the idea of God as being literally timeless were discussed. According to this view, time never passes for God and there is, therefore, no before or after; no past, present or future. Instead all things are present simultaneously to God. The attractions of this view are considerable, as then God knows the future in exactly the same way as the past and the present, since all events are simultaneously present to him. St Augustine considered that time began at the creation of the world, and he said that God had 'the complete possession of eternal life all at once'. Boethius gave the best-known formulation of this idea when he said that God had 'the whole, simultaneous and perfect possession of eternal life'. St Thomas Aquinas followed closely in this tradition (see (2) below).

However, as we shall see later, there are considerable difficulties with the idea of God as being outside time, and questions arise as to whether such a God can love, know or, indeed, act in any way. David Hume in his *Dialogues* has his character Cleanthes express the position thus:

A mind whose acts and sentiments and ideas are not distinct and successive, one that is wholly simple and totally immutable, is a mind which has no Thought, no Reason, no Will, no Sentiment, no Love, no Hatred; or in a word is no mind at all. It is an abuse of terms to give it that appelation.

The idea of God as timeless can, therefore, be challenged and he can instead be regarded as EVERLASTING – in other words he has no beginning and no end but endures everlastingly into the past and the future. Such a God may experience time differently from us (for instance 'a thousand ages in his sight may be but an evening gone'), but time still passes for him. The future is still future and the past is past.

Einstein's theory of relativity has shown that there is no cosmic 'now' – time is relative for all of us. Indeed if we could travel in a space-ship at close to the speed of light, time would slow down. This leads to the famous 'twins-paradox'. Imagine two twins, one of whom sets out in a spaceship capable of travelling at very close to the speed of light and she travels to the other side of our galaxy and back again. Her twin remains on earth. Einstein showed that, according to the theory of relativity, the earth-bound twin would have been dead for possibly hundreds of years when her twin returned to earth, yet the travelling twin would have aged by, possibly, only ten years or so. In other words time passes differently for the two individuals. Similarly time may pass differently for God – but it still passes. God may know the future with considerable or complete accuracy, but he will still know it as future.

This approach sees God as personal – he is in some sense an individual who can know, love, think and reason in a somewhat similar fashion to man. Certainly God is a spirit, but nevertheless he is an individual Spirit with whom the believer can have a two-way relationship. God can respond to man as a father responds to his children. He can act and react. He can even change his mind. This approach can, therefore, be thought of as closest to the ideas of the biblical writers who thought of God in these terms. On this view, the biblical writers wrote literally when talking of God. They intended their words to have the same force as words have in our common understanding of them.

Plato considered that anything that was in time is subject to change and, therefore, cannot be perfect or complete. This is not necessarily the case. The Christian would want to maintain that Jesus was perfect and that he was equally perfect on his thirtieth and on his thirty-first birthdays. During the intervening year time certainly passed for Jesus. The passage of time would not, however, affect Jesus' moral perfection which depended not on his being immutable (which he clearly was not) but on his having a perfect character and therefore reacting perfectly to every situation in which he found himself. However Plato's idea of perfection goes beyond mere moral perfection to an idea of metaphysical perfection – a form of completeness which cannot change. God is as he is and cannot be other than he is. If this view is denied, God can still be thought of as morally perfect and changeless in his character and in his love for his people. His love is the same yesterday, today and tomorrow. He will not have bad moods or change his mind about his care for us, even though time passes. This still leaves open, however, the possibility of his metaphysical perfection changing; in other words, through interaction with the world, there could be some development allowed for God, albeit a development which does not have to affect his character or dispositions.

If God is in time, then clearly God did not create time.

13

Some of the early Church Fathers considered this to be a problem as, if God was within time, surely there was something greater than God, i.e. time itself. However, time need not be looked on as a 'thing' which needs to be created. Time is a feature of anything that exists; if God existed before the creation of the universe, then time would exist because God existed. Time would always have existed just as God would always have existed. At a certain moment in time, God would have created the world and he would then have seen his purposes unfolding in his creation. In other words, the presence of time does not have to be seen as any limitation of God.

There are difficulties with this view. God is seen as relatively anthropomorphic and may be regarded as something like a 'superman' or even as rather like the 'old man with a white beard'. This may not reflect the required degree of perfection and transcendence which some believers consider necessary for God. It assumes that when the Bible says that man was made in the image of God this is to be taken literally and not metaphorically. Indeed on this view most language about God is used in a similar, if expanded manner to the way language is used on earth (i.e. it is used 'univocally' – see next section). There are also problems with the extent to which God can know the future. Certainly, according to this view, he may have foreknowledge, in that he knows the future as future (this does not apply to a timeless God who perceives everything simultaneously) but he may not necessarily know the future in detail. This need not be seen as limiting God, however, as it may be held that a personal and everlasting God has chosen not to know the outcome of our free choices. He might not, therefore, have known in 1066 that the Vietnam war would take place. Whether this limits God is a matter about which philosophers differ.

'Process theologians', who are influential particularly in the United States, have taken this view of God considerably further and maintain that God is 'in process'. Through God interacting with his creation, he is developing and changing. God and the universe are closely linked, and developments in the world bring about real change in God. Process theology emphasises God's relationship with his creation and the centrality of God's love for his creatures. God develops, in a somewhat analogous way to man developing, by interaction with the universe and the people he has created. All relationships entail development and, if God can enter into relationship with individuals, it necessarily follows that he changes as the relationships progress. Instead of the traditional Catholic emphasis on God as 'Being', Process Theology emphasises God's 'becoming'.

Process theologians would strongly reject what they regard as the static picture of God provided by the view of God as timeless substance set out in the next section. They see this view resulting from scholastic metaphysics and they appeal to a relatively literal reading of some parts of the Bible in support of their position. One of the problems with such an appeal is, however, that it is based on certain preconceptions about how the Bible is to be interpreted and these preconceptions may not be shared by others. An appeal to the Bible will not by itself decide the issue.

Process Theology sees God and the universe as interdependent. Traditionally Christianity has rejected this view by emphasising that God created the world from nothing – thus showing the tremendous gulf that separates God and man and the fact that while the universe without God is nothing, God without the universe is still fully God. Those who maintain that God is everlasting could accept this view and are not, therefore, committed to going as far as process theologians do in affirming that God and the world are interdependent.

There is, thus, no need for the view of God as personal and everlasting to be taken as far as process theologians want to take it and there can be a sliding scale about which legitimate debate is possible as to how far a God who is in time must and can change and develop. Nevertheless, wherever on this sliding scale an individual's view is to be located, he or she will still see God as a personal agent who is everlasting.

This view of God is probably the most widespread amongst ordinary believers who are not theologically or philosophically sophisticated. They consider that they experience God as an individual and maintain that they can have a two-way relationship with him in prayer. God can be addressed as 'Thou' as part of a two-way 'I-Thou' relationship on similar lines to a relationship between two individuals. Many theologians and philosophers, however, consider that this

15

approach is inadequate and would maintain that one of the other alternatives set out below comes closer to a true understanding of what is meant by God.

2 God as timeless substance

St Thomas Aquinas was, without question, the single most influential theologian in the Roman Catholic Church. At the Council of Trent (1546) St Thomas' writings together with the Bible and the decrees of the popes were the only books left on the altar that from them 'might be sought counsel, reasons and answers' (Pope Leo XIII's papal bull of 1879). St Thomas' influence has been enormous and is still very much with us.

Aquinas lived between 1225 and 1274 at a time when the writings of Aristotle had recently been rediscovered. Some of the early Church Fathers had, as we have seen, been influenced by Plato, but Aristotle's writings had been lost in the West and had, therefore, little influence on the development of early Christian ideas. These writings were, however, maintained in the East and affected the work of Islamic philosophers and theologians. When they were reintroduced to the West they had a profound influence. Aquinas brought together Aristotle's ideas with those of the Early Church. His great achievement was to recognise frankly and honestly many of the difficulties that Christianity faced in making itself understood, and he attempted to deal with these difficulties, often with the aid of Aristotle's philosophy.

The Muslim philosopher Ibn al-Arabi, as well as other Christian and Islamic writers prior to Aquinas, had said that we can know nothing at all about what God is like – only what he is not. We can know nothing about God at all and there is no way we can arrive at any knowledge of God. Thus Ibn al-Arabi said:

It is important that you know Him after this fashion, not by learning, not by intellect, not by understanding, not by imagination, not by sense, not by the outward eye, not by the inward eye, not by perception . . . His veil that is phenomenal existence is but the concealment of His exist-

ence in His Oneness, without any attribute. (Quoted from
Margaret Smith's *Readings from the Mystics of Islam*, p. 118)

The problem with a long list of negative statements is that
one ends up by saying nothing at all. This idea of the VIA
NEGATIVA (literally the 'negative way' of talking only in terms
of what God is not) was very influential, but Aquinas did not
accept it. He recognised that Christians had talked in great
detail about God, and so he sought to set out what this
theological language meant. He did recognise that there were
some negative statements that we could correctly make about
God (for instance that God is not in time and does not change
in any way), but these were restricted. Nevertheless this class
of negative statements was tremendously important, as
Aquinas maintained that only these negative statements could
be known to be literally true about God. When, therefore,
God is described as spaceless and timeless these are to be
taken *as literally true statements*. Very few statements about God
are to be taken in this way but, for Aquinas, it is literally
true that time does not pass for God. This is crucial, as the
whole of this view of God depends on his timelessness being
taken as literally true.

Aquinas considered that we could not know what God was
like in himself since God was wholly other than us. He said
that any language (whether religious or otherwise) could be
used in one of two ways – neither of which he considered
appropriate to God. Words could either be used:

(a) UNIVOCALLY. A word is used univocally if it has the same
meaning in two different cases. Thus if we say that God is
good, a man is good and a dog is good, the word 'good' would
be used 'univocally' if in all three cases the meaning of 'good'
is similar. Aquinas denied that words can be used univocally
of God. Thus, when the believer says that God is good, loving,
caring, etc., these words do *not* mean the same as when they
are used of human beings.

(b) EQUIVOCALLY. A word is used equivocally if its meaning
is totally different in two different cases. Thus if we say that
'the Queen is the ruler' and 'I have a ruler on my desk', the
word 'ruler' is used in entirely different senses. If I know

what it is for the Queen to be a ruler this will tell me nothing at all about what it is for me to have a ruler on my desk. If, therefore, words are used equivocally of God, then they have an entirely different meaning when applied to God as compared with the way they are used in the ordinary world. Literally, therefore, we do not know what words mean when they are applied to God if they are regarded as equivocal. This option, also, Aquinas rejected.

In order to overcome this problem, Aquinas developed a theory of analogy and metaphor. The exact meaning of Aquinas' ideas on analogy has been much debated, but effectively he maintained that although we may be able to use words correctly about God, we cannot know what it would be for these words to be true when they are applied to God. If, therefore, we had analogy alone to work with, the believer would end up using language about God which he could maintain was correctly applied to God, but the content and meaning he would give to this language would be very limited indeed. The believer would, thus, be limited to a very restricted view indeed of what God was like.

Human beings have the potential to be and to do many things; they have enormous potential in many areas which they may or may not actualise. All things in the universe have the potential to be something else. Matter can be transformed into energy, energy can in turn be transformed in many different ways – everything has potential. God, however, is in a different category as if he had any potential which he had not realised, he would not be fully perfect. As God is totally unchanging and outside time (in this view of God), he is wholly perfect, he has and can have no potentiality at all – he is 'pure act' or pure actuality. He is fully whatever it is to be God and he cannot be other than what he is. As he is timeless, he cannot change. So we have the picture of God as fully actual, God as 'pure actuality', God as fully God – albeit without us being able to know what it is for God to be God.

The last paragraph may appear complex but is less difficult than it seems at first. Effectively all the believer can say literally (apart from a limited number of negative statements referred to above) is that God is fully whatever it is to be

God and he cannot be anything other than this. The most, indeed, that the believer can say with any precision about God is that 'God is' – there is no way that the further step can be taken to say what he is. Obviously this view leaves the believer with a restricted view of what the God is whom he or she is worshipping.

Most of the language in the Bible which applies to God is, according to this view, metaphorical. This does not mean that the language is not true, but it does mean that it is not literally true. The Bible provides helpful pictures of God's activity, but since we cannot know anything at all about what God is like in himself or what it is for God to 'act', we cannot know what it means for this language to be true. This language may, however, be helpful for the believer when he or she thinks about God and it may, indeed, be true. To take an example, when the Bible says that Abraham stood before the Lord and asked him not to destroy Sodom for the sake of first fifty, then forty-five, then forty and, eventually, ten righteous men who might be in the City (Gen. 18), this (in the view of God as an everlasting individual) would mean that God changed his mind. If God is timeless, however, he cannot change his mind since he cannot change in any way. It follows that 'God repented of the action' would be taken as metaphorical. It is not literally true.

In the previous chapter, we saw that the Bible required interpretation; few believers, it was suggested as an example, take the Genesis story literally. The story is meant to convey a message and this message can be true without the story itself being literally true. Some independent standpoint is required from which the biblical material can be interpreted and, in this view, this standpoint rests on God's timelessness. Once this has been accepted, then the Bible can be seen as conveying truths about God, albeit not literal truths. God is so 'other than' us, so different from us that we cannot know what he is like in himself. The most we can have is an impression of his activity in the world which is described in biblical stories which need interpretation and must not be taken literally.

Aquinas therefore considered that some (few) things could be said literally about God and these included the view that he was timeless and spaceless – strictly outside time and space. The origins of the idea of timelessness lay in Plato's philosophy but also in the ideas of St Augustine and Boethius. We therefore have the situation that:

- We cannot know what God is like in himself.
- We do know, however, that he is literally timeless and spaceless.
- We can correctly talk of God as 'loving', 'caring', 'acting' etc., but since we do not know what God is, we cannot know what it means for these words to be true of God. Certainly, however, they do not mean the same as when these words are used in ordinary language. To say that 'God loves me' is *not* equivalent, even on a much magnified scale, to saying 'my wife loves me'.
- God is 'pure act' in that he has no potential and cannot be other than he is.
- Most biblical statements about God are metaphorical; they should not be taken as literally true, but their 'force' or the impact of the story they are telling is nevertheless true.

According to this view, God's transcendence is emphasised. We may have to use anthropomorphic language about God, but we need to recognise that this cannot tell us what God is like in himself. God is in no sense an anthropomorphic figure. He is outside time, so all events that have ever occurred or will ever occur are simultaneously present to him. He therefore knows what you will pray on your deathbed, what you are doing now and what was happening in the depths of space ten million years ago – all simultaneously. There is no before or after for God but one single glorious cosmic 'now' in which everything is equally present to him. This view is obviously very different from the first option we considered and will have a major effect on what the believer considers happens in prayer or after death (amongst other topics that we shall consider later).

This view is closest to that of many Catholic theologians and philosophers for whom Aquinas and the views of the early Church Fathers have been a major influence. Philosophically it has many attractions: God's transcendence is emphasised; he knows everything in the past, present and future and so is truly omniscient; and there is no risk of his being reduced to our level. Amongst the problems is that we do not really know what it means to say that 'God is' and there is a strong element of mystery and agnosticism in this view. (AGNOSTICISM = recognising that we cannot know about something. An agnostic in religious terms is generally taken to be someone who does not know whether or not God exists.) In this context, God is certainly held to exist but the believer does not know what it is that exists.

3 The linguistic view of God

Philosophers have long been concerned about what it means for us to 'know' something to be true. Many considered that in order for us to know anything, something must be certain. Language had to have foundations which were INDUBITABLE (i.e. could not be doubted) if we were to know anything at all. Various candidates have been suggested for these foundations – the two most influential of these in modern times have been put forward by:

René Descartes. Descartes looked for something that he could be absolutely certain about. He considered that unless there was some such thing about which he could be certain, then he would have no reason to be sure of anything. He looked inside himself and came up with the one thing that could not be doubted – this was the famous '*Cogito*' (from '*Cogito Ergo Sum*', Latin for 'I think therefore I am'). Given that he (Descartes) was a thinking thing, he could not doubt his own existence. For Descartes, therefore, the content of his mind was that about which he was most certain. Given this one statement that he could be sure about, Descartes then set out to show that on this foundation he could justify claims to know other things, based largely on his having 'clear and distinct ideas' about them.

One of the problems with this approach is that truth depends on an interior test. Inner certainty and truth are brought together and it becomes very difficult to separate true and false knowledge claims. This was one (of many) reasons why Descartes' approach was rejected.

John Locke. Locke considered that the things we could be

certain about were those that we experience. He was an
EMPIRICIST (literally someone who relies on experience) and
the primary experiences that we have of things provided
Locke's foundations for knowledge.

St Thomas, one of Jesus' twelve Apostles, was also an
empiricist when he said to the disciples: 'Unless I see in his
hands the print of the nails, and place my finger in the mark
of the nails, and place my hand in his side, I will not believe'
(John 20:25). In other words, Thomas is demanding empirical
evidence of the resurrection of Jesus from the dead. Amongst
the problems with this view is that all experiences that we
have require interpretation – we can tell the difference
between a real oasis and a mirage because of our ability to
interpret. The experience itself does not carry within itself a
guarantee of correctness.

The whole idea that knowledge rests on some form of
indubitable foundations – whether internal (Descartes) or
based on experience (Locke) – has come in for sustained
attack throughout this century. Two of the most influential
philosophers challenging this position were G. E. Moore and,
particularly, L. Wittgenstein. These two men showed that
language is a public affair and that we are educated into the
use of language. Language makes contact with the world
through certain simple, banal statements that it really does
not make sense to doubt such as 'This is a chair', 'Here is a
pen', 'That is a bookcase', etc. You really cannot justify these
propositions. Imagine a child continually asking his mother
'Why?', 'Why?', 'Why?' and eventually, after hearing the
patient replies of the mother, the child asks, for instance,
'Why is that a chair?' to which the mother (more or less
patiently) replies: 'Because that is simply the name we give
to that sort of thing.' There is no other explanation and no
other justification.

Instead of trying to arrive at statements that we can be
absolutely certain about, Wittgenstein pioneered a completely
new way of approaching philosophy. He rejected any attempt
to look for foundations for knowledge and showed that, when
a child grows up in a society, he is educated into a public
language and a public form of life. The child comes to accept
the meaning given to words like 'chair', 'pen' and 'bookcase'

without any attempt to justify these words in terms of some basic foundations of knowledge. In short, the whole idea that knowledge rested on foundations was seen to be misconceived.

Wittgenstein's approach to philosophy 'left everything as it was' in that he simply looked at the language people used to try to understand how it was applied. When Wittgenstein looked at the things religious believers said, he came to the conclusion that they were not making the same type of claims as scientists make. For instance their claims were not predictions about what would happen in the future and the believers allowed no evidence to count against their claims. The believer bases his or her life on claims that cannot be justified by normal methods, and even the things he or she says seem to have little to do with the way things turn out in the world. Thus when believers talk of God being good, loving and all-powerful, they will not change their minds about these claims even if they become bankrupt, their house burns down, their children are killed in an accident and they contract cancer (Job is a good biblical example of this). *Whatever* happens, believers will still maintain that God loves them.

Wittgenstein gives an example of talking about the Last Judgement. If a believer asks if he (Wittgenstein) believes in a Last Judgement, Wittgenstein says that he might try to define what it is that the believer means. However, *whatever* definition Wittgenstein gives, the believer says, 'No, I don't mean that'. Finally Wittgenstein is left at a loss for words – he simply does not understand what the believer is saying, he cannot contradict the believer and must simply accept that the believer is operating with a different language which he, as an outsider, cannot understand. Given this situation, all the outsider can do is to look at the role which the language used by the believer plays in his or her life.

Language is rather like a game. You can look at a children's game and can learn the rules of the game by observation. Similarly by looking at the way believers use religious language you may come to a conclusion about how this language is being used and what meaning it has for the believer.

Wittgenstein considered part of his task was to set limits to the use of language; to set limits to what could and could not be said. He maintained, with regret, that all the most important things in life lay beyond the limits of what could be expressed in language. The religious believer is not, in Wittgenstein's view, making claims about anything METAPHYSICAL (the derived meaning of which is 'beyond physics', i.e. things that go beyond the world we experience or which science can deal with). In order to understand just what the believer *is* doing we must look at the role that religious language plays in the believer's life.

Wittgenstein has been very influential and has spawned a sea of disciples, of whom the most important (although by no means the sole) writer in the field of religion is Dewi Phillips who has written a series of books which take this position to its logical conclusion. It is open to debate as to what extent Phillips and other philosophers who have been strongly influenced by Wittgenstein have been faithful to Wittgenstein's own ideas and to what extent they have developed their own ideas. This, however, is not an issue that we shall be exploring here.

There are various ways in which this view can be expressed but, effectively, God is real and God exists as a reality within the language of the religious community alone. Within the religious language game God necessarily exists. To the religious believer, God's existence is undoubted – but it is an existence enshrined in and preserved by the language of religion. It is very important not to immediately jump to the conclusion that this is denying that God exists. Frequently people who have read a little about this position will say, 'Oh, but supporters of this view do not really believe that God exists at all'. This is not the case. Certainly God exists in this view; God is really real and really existent! It depends, of course, on what you mean by 'real' and 'exists'. We might imagine a conversation between an advocate of this view and an opponent which went as follows:

LINGUISTIC PHILOSOPHER: Within the believing community, within the religious language game, God exists and God is real.

OPPONENT: But you are denying the existence of God. In your view God only exists within language. He does not really exist.

L. P.: What do you mean 'really exist'? Are you saying that

God is an object like a chair or a planet? Because if you
are then I think you are talking nonsense.

o.: No, of course God is not an object like that, but he exists
apart from the universe he has created.

L. P.: I don't understand what you mean. The universe is the
totality of all that is. Are you saying God is an object
outside this universe? Again, if you are saying this, then I
don't think this is a reflection of traditional Christianity.
Christianity maintains that God is transcendent (he is
beyond our normal experience of the universe), but he is
also imminent in all that the believer experiences of the
world. I would accept this and my view allows for it.

o.: But in your view what account can be given of all the
things that religious people believe in – prayer, miracles,
eternal life, religious experience? You have to dismiss all
these.

L. P.: Not at all. All these are a vital part of religious language
and I want to affirm the value of such theological talk and
to show its meaning. Theological language cannot and must
not be reduced to any other form of language. It preserves
insights into the human condition which are not available
elsewhere and the believer, by relating his life wholly to
the reality that is God, finds a meaning and purpose which
would not otherwise be there.

Just what meaning the linguistic philosopher would give to
religious talk we shall see in later chapters, but his view can
be a profound and relatively comprehensive one.

In some ways this view can be seen as an extension beyond
the view of God as timeless. It is the result of the progressive
abstraction that has taken place in man's ideas of God. God
can no longer (in this view) be thought of as a spiritual being
or thing. Instead, the existent reality that is God is found
within the believing community. As Jesus said, 'Whenever
two or three are gathered together in my name, I will be
there with them.' The believer, once he or she has understood
what the term God means, can never be separated from the
reality that is God.

There could be a parallel with the idea of prime numbers
(as Norman Malcolm helpfully suggested in a paper on the
ontological argument for the existence of God). Imagine you

are a mathematician and you have a use for the idea of prime numbers. Indeed, not only do you have a use for this idea, but prime numbers have a vital role to play in all your calculations. Someone may say to you, 'But prime numbers do not exist!' You would reply, 'Of course they do, let me show you.' You may attempt to show them the reality of prime numbers, the value they have for you and how your working life is centred around their use. If, in the end, you cannot make them see what prime numbers are, this does not affect their reality – the numbers 1, 2, 3, 5, 7, 11, 13, etc. *are* prime numbers. Similarly with the believer. Once the believer has a use for the idea of God, once the idea of God exists for him and is a reality for him, once he relates his whole life to God, then it will not make sense for the believer to doubt that God exists. What is more, he or she will never be able to get away from the reality of God. To amend Ps. 139:9 one could say: 'If I take the wings of the morning and dwell in the uttermost parts of the sea, even there prime numbers shall be with me.' Substitute God for prime numbers and you have the similar point. Nothing can separate the believer from the reality of God which he or she has found within the believing community and to which he or she is relating his or her life. The effects of this reality are seen within religious language and we shall discuss them in detail in due course.

4 Talk of God seen as affirming a possible way in which life can be lived

This view is not as well known as that set out above, but it lies in a long tradition starting from Plato. Indeed the view can be looked on as Platonic. The foremost modern exponent is Stewart Sutherland in his book *God, Jesus and Belief* (Blackwell 1984) and this section owes a great deal to his views.

John Robinson, in *Honest to God*, followed partly in the steps of Paul Tillich when he said that our traditional idea of God had to go. Tillich, writing in a famous meditation 'The Depth of Existence' and considering the road to wisdom found in all continents and ages, said of the depth that is God:

> The name of this infinite and inexhaustible depth . . . is GOD. That depth is what the word GOD means. And if that word has not much meaning for you, translate it and speak of the depths of your life . . . Perhaps, in order to do so, you must forget everything traditional that you have learned about God . . . (Tillich, *The Shaking of the foundations*, p. 57)

This idea of God as depth or the depth of your life has been particularly influential. More recently Don Cupitt has put forward, in *Taking Leave of God*, ideas which take this rejection of the traditional view a stage further. Both Robinson's and Cupitt's books are well worth reading, and both have had a considerable impact. Sutherland's views owe little to Tillich, Robinson or Cupitt but he, also, rejects the traditional idea of God, and his ideas are part of a long tradition that has considerable explanatory power. In some ways they can be seen as taking this approach to God to its logical conclusion, so it is his ideas that will mainly be used here.

Sutherland starts by rejecting the traditional ideal of God as in some sense a Being or Spirit whether as everlasting individual or as timeless substance. He argues that Christian ideas have developed over time and, if God is thought of in these terms, the idea of God can be shown to be incoherent. In particular, Sutherland maintains that believers have never succeeded in solving the problem of evil (which revolves round the dilemma that an all-powerful and all-good God is meant to have made a world which contains much evil – see ch. 7). It is time, Sutherland maintains, to recognise the inadequacy of previous conceptions of God and to move beyond these to a new view which makes sense and yet preserves the distinctive character of religion. Again, therefore, we have a philosopher who is not arguing for the rejection of religion or of God but is instead maintaining that talk of God is valid and the religious way of life makes sense. However, to understand what he means it is first necessary to understand what he means by God.

When the gospel writers record that Jesus was tempted in the wilderness, few people today, it is argued, consider that an individual called 'the Devil' was involved. Jesus had gone away into the wilderness to reflect on his life and his future.

Various alternatives were open to him and he had to make real decisions that would affect the rest of his life. As Sutherland says, he wrestled with what was real and not with a delusion – he could genuinely have followed various paths in the future. If believers are willing to accept that Jesus was thus wrestling in the wilderness with the dark side of his character and the possibility of living a life that was other than the one he finally chose, why cannot the same be said of his experiences in the Garden of Gethsemane? Just as there was no 'Devil' thought of as some spiritual individual in the wilderness, so it does not make sense to think of some 'spiritual Father' to whom Jesus prayed in Gethsemane. However, the alternatives open to Jesus were only too real – he had major decisions to make in Gethsemane. He could see the certain prospect on the following day of a hideous death. Still, at this final stage, he could avoid it. He could avoid his crucifixion and follow some other path. The choice was his. The temptation must have been very great but, in the end, by praying quietly he came to recognise that this was not the right way forward. If he was to be true to himself, if he was to remain faithful to what he had preached throughout his life, then he must go through with his forthcoming arrest and crucifixion – he must not try to escape.

There are choices available in any human life, and great religious figures such as Jesus have shown, through talk of God, that it is possible for an individual to live a good and selfless life even though this may mean suffering and death. From the world's point of view these men seem to have lost everything, but the saints, mystics and martyrs affirm that this is not the case. It is possible to live a selfless life committed to God and not be mad.

Sutherland makes a major claim about his view which shows his close affinity to Plato. He says that talk of God, talk of the possibility of living a good life, involves an ONTOLOGICAL COMMITMENT. This means that to say that talk of God is meaningful, that the religous life is of value and that martyrdom and sacrifice are worthwhile are statements about the nature of reality. The universe is such that a good and saintly life can be lived and is a possibility available for rational beings. Talk of God, therefore, is talk of an alternative way in which life can be lived.

It is important to notice that this is a much larger claim than the linguistic view (set out in section 3) which saw the reality of God's existence lying within religious language. Carried to its logical conclusion the linguistic view means that, in the absence of language, God does not exist. If there were no religious believers there would be no God. Sutherland's view goes much further than this. For Sutherland, the universe is such that a good and saintly life is possible. If men were wiped out, if there were no religious believers and no talk of God, this possible way of living life would still remain. Even if the planet Earth was existinguished and a race of intelligent green spiders emerged on one of the planets of a far-flung star, the possible way of living which is affirmed by talk of God would remain to be discovered.

This view cannot be reduced to morality. A critic might say, 'But all you are saying is that a good life is possible. We can use the language of morality to explain all religious terms. Morality can, indeed, move over to explain religion.' This is *not* the case. Religious language and talk of God *cannot* thus be reduced to morality on this view; religion preserves the possibility for looking at the world in a different way. Sutherland terms this the possibility of looking at the world '*sub specie aeternitatis*' (under or from the auspices of the eternal). He does not mean by this that there is any eternal realm from which the world can be regarded, but rather that any moral system can be expanded and influenced by a religious outlook which, indeed, can show that existing ideas of morality are inadequate. Thus a Wilberforce can reject the morality of his time which accepted slavery and can appeal to a religious view of life (a view of life *sub specie aeternitatis*) to show that society's morality was inadequate and must be changed.

The very real attraction of this view is that all religions, in their talk of God, Allah, Jehovah, etc. can be seen to be affirming the possibility of a different way of looking at and living life. They can all be seen to be challenging the normal conception of the world's priorities and saying that an individual can live in an entirely different way, a way that the world may regard as foolish, that may bring no apparent results except for opposition, suffering and persecution, and yet is a way that is fulfilling, meaningful and fundamentally worthwhile.

If, therefore, this view is accepted, all religions can be seen to be aiming at a same objective. In a world in which religious intolerance is still very real and the cause of bitter conflict in many areas, this may be looked on as a most important development in the field of religion and education as well as, indeed, any Church's idea of its missionary role.

5 Summary

We have, therefore, four conceptions of God:

(1) God as personal and everlasting;
(2) God as timeless substance;
(3) the linguistic view of God;
(4) talk of God seen as affirming a possible way in which life can be lived.

All of these are important, all are influential, all have great explanatory power and all suffer from real weaknesses in different areas. Whichever view you take is going to have a great impact on what you can say (and even more on what you mean) in most of the main areas with which religious believers are concerned. We must now turn to the first of these areas and will see how the view that is taken of God will shape and determine what any believer means and what he can say.

4

Miracles

John Traynor was severely wounded in the First World War. Both his legs were paralysed and he could not walk. He had severed nerves in the right upper arm, and even after four operations he was still unable to move his right hand. He had a hole over an inch in diameter in his head in which a silver plate was inserted and he had frequent epileptic fits. The Ministry of War Pensions certified him as 100 per cent disabled and he used to sit all day in the front room of his little house in Liverpool. Traynor had always had a great devotion to the Virgin Mary and in 1923 he decided to use the last of his savings to go to Lourdes – against the will of his local Catholic priest as well as his doctor who said that the journey would kill him. On his final night in Lourdes he was fully cured and was able to get up and run down to the shrine to give thanks. He could walk properly and use his arm again. The hole in his head healed over leaving only a slight indentation. The medical board at Lourdes found no evidence of epilepsy or paralysis. His right arm was no longer atrophied, his pectoral and shoulder muscles were restored and bone had grown over the hole in his head. The official report declared: 'This extraordinary cure is absolutely beyond and above the powers of nature.' Thousands greeted Traynor on his return to Liverpool. He went into the haulage business and ran a small fleet of lorries. He died twenty years later of a hernia unconnected with his war wounds.

This report of John Traynor's miraculous healing is an example of the classic idea of what a miracle is. In some way God has intervened to do something which is against the laws of nature. The miracle stories in the Bble belong to the oldest part of the biblical tradition and, for instance, more than half of Mark's Gospel revolves around miracle stories. For the

31

believer to reject claims to miracle is, therefore, a very major step indeed – particularly as the resurrection is claimed to be the greatest miracle of all.

To regard a miracle as a breach of the laws of nature is, however, by no means the only possible description of a miracle and it is important to be clear on the options.

The main possibilities are:

1 A miracle is a violation of the laws of nature by an action of God (examples include Jesus walking on water or Traynor's cure).
2 A miracle is an act by God intervening in the world but which nevertheless does not go against the laws of nature.
3 A miracle is a particular event or circumstance which one or more religious believers see as having religious significance or as being due to God's action but which can also be explained on other grounds. (It will be obvious that the dividing line between (2) and (3) is by no means clear cut.)
4 A miracle as a transformation which takes place within a human being which, although not being against any law of nature, is nevertheless so improbable as to be totally surprising and remarkable and is therefore considered to have religious significance.
5 A miracle as an unusual event or happening which does not have religious significance (for instance the rescue of a baby from the ruins of a city hit by an earthquake more than seven days after the earthquake occurred).

Option (5) can be eliminated from our discussion as, although it may be described in colloquial terms as a 'miracle', it does not have the religious significance which is usually associated with this word. This leaves four main possibilities which we shall now consider.

1 Miracle as a violation of laws of nature

The strongest and still the most effective attack on the first idea of miracle was made by David Hume in his *Dialogues*. Hume rejects the whole idea of reports of miracles considered as breaches of the laws of nature on the grounds that it will always be more probable that the reports of a miracle are mistaken than that a law of nature has been breached. To paraphrase David Hume, he says the following:

> A wise man proportions his belief to the evidence. A miracle is the violation of the laws of nature and is therefore an event which past human experience is uniformly against. This in itself makes it overwhelmingly probable that the miracle did not occur, unless the testimony to it is of such superlative quality that it can seriously be weighed against our uniform past experience. In fact, however, the testimony to miracles is not of this character at all; the standard of the witnesses has not been high, the human capacity for accepting or believing the unlikely has all too probably been at work, the tales related derive from 'ignorant and barbarous places and nations' and, in any case, the miracle stories of different religions contradict each other. Consequently testimony to miracles can never establish them so that one could proceed from a proper assurance that they occurred to infer some theistic conclusion.

This is a very famous statement and it is worth analysing the claims that Hume is making. Hume argues that:

(a) A miracle is a breach of a law of nature.

(b) Belief in miracles is not rational. Rationality, Hume maintains, involves:
  – proportioning your belief to the evidence available;
  – the uniform past evidence we have for laws of nature (if this were not the case we would not consider that we were dealing with a law since laws of nature do not admit exceptions); and
  – the fact that we do not have uniform evidence for the accuracy of human testimony. It is often untrustworthy, people lie and can be sincerely mistaken.
  So it will always be more rational to believe that laws of nature hold than that a miracle occurred. It will always be more rational to believe that when someone tries to walk on water they will sink than to believe a report that one man tried this and succeeded.

(c) Not only is belief in miracles (defined as breaches of laws of nature) irrational, but the testimony available is poor. Thus:

 – The testimony of witnesses. Hume requires that witnesses should be educated and intelligent. They should have a reputation to lose and nothing to gain. It could be argued, for instance, that in the case of the New Testament miracle stories, relatively ignorant fishermen had a great deal to gain from miracle stories attributed to the man they were following who had been put to death.

 – Human nature loves the fantastic. People love the idea of something unlikely happening. Reports of UFOs are very common and many people still claim to see the Loch Ness monster.

 – Reports of miracles come from ignorant and barbarous people. Primitive folk-lore has many tales of miracles and strange stories of the supernatural.

 If, therefore, the poor testimony to miracles is put together with the unlikelihood that laws of nature would be breached, it will always be more sensible to reject reports of miracles than to believe them.

(d) All religions claim miracles, so all religions have equal claims to truth if one bases the truth of religions on the miracle stories. Assuming that different religions are not compatible, the miracle stories from different traditions simply cancel out and provide, as Hume puts it, a 'complete triumph for the sceptic'.

There are a number of weaknesses with these criticisms of Hume's, and although they look compelling on the surface they are much less so when analysed in detail.

Firstly, Christianity has never claimed that someone should believe on the basis of miracles. Jesus himself rejected any appeal to signs and wonders as evidence for his status. He acknowledged that others would do miracles as well. When, therefore, one considers whether or not belief in miracles is rational, one should not be looking at them as an uncommited observer. Instead the question should be whether, given that an individual is a believer on other grounds, belief in miracles

34

is then rational. This is to put the matter in quite a different light. If someone already believes in God then (subject to what he or she means by 'God' as we shall discuss below) belief in miracles is not irrational. What is *not* reasonable, as Hume rightly argues, is to base belief on reports of miracles.

Secondly, Hume was writing at a time when attestation to miracles was almost entirely by word of mouth and when science was in its infancy. It is difficult to know what he would make of the well documented case of someone like John Traynor. Here the witnesses were doctors and scientists who had a good deal to lose, the evidence was documented in the form of the reports of a number of doctors and X-ray photographs and, in short, the evidence largely measures up to the standards that Hume set. Hume, being a Scot, might have liked one of the doctors to have been a Scot, but provided this nationalistic bias is ignored, then the evidence seems good!

Thirdly, Hume only deals with reports of miracles. Nothing in his argument succeeds in showing that one should ignore a miracle that one has experienced oneself.

Fourthly, he emphasises 'laws of nature' as if they were set in stone, thus implying that no law of nature can be shown to be incorrect. If any evidence is produced which counts against an existing law of nature one would have to ignore it. This is certainly incorrect because, as science develops, so our understanding of laws of nature increases and what were previously considered to be 'laws' are seen to be only inadequate approximations. To be fair to Hume, he could restate his point here and maintain that one should only take account of evidence against a supposed law of nature if this evidence could be produced under laboratory conditions and had predictive power. In other words one should ignore purported isolated exceptions to laws of nature and should only recognise exceptions if an experiment could be produced and repeated as required to show that the supposed law did not hold. However the possibility of what we regard as laws of nature being shown to be incorrect must always remain open.

This, in fact, leads to an even more potent attack on the idea of miracle as a breach of laws of nature. Even if a remarkable event (such as Traynor's cure) takes place, it is still perfectly reasonable to accept that the event happened but to reject the idea that God was involved. Perhaps we are instead dealing with a remarkable power of the human mind which we do not yet understand. Surely, it can be argued, we should remain open to this possibility? A hundred years ago television, radio and air travel would have been regarded as miraculous but we know that they are merely based on superior technology that was not available in the nineteenth century. So in all cases of reported miracles, the idea of God does not need to be brought in. This seems an entirely reasonable view to take and much will depend on the individual's prior view as to whether or not God exists or what idea of God he or she is working with. If the individual is a believer in a personal God who acts in the world, then there is no reason why belief in miracles (as defined under (1) in this chapter) should be regarded as unreasonable or irrational. If, however, an individual does not believe in God, then there is no good reason why the report of a 'miracle' should induce this belief.

Belief in miracles seen as breaches of laws of nature cannot, therefore, be ruled out. However we must now introduce the four different concepts of God discussed in chapter 2. If someone works with the idea of God as an everlasting, personal individual, then there is no reason why they should not also believe in miracles as representing actions by this God against the laws of nature as they are perceived by us. If, however, they take the linguistic view of God or they consider that talk of God is affirming the possibility of a different way of living life, then miracles as breaches of laws of nature must be ruled out. They cannot happen since there is no God of the sort that could act to carry out a miracle.

A more complicated problem arises with the second conception of God as timeless substance. The issue here goes to the very heart of this idea of God and depends on whether such a God can do anything at all – whether, in other words, a timeless God can act. God, in this view, is strictly outside time. Time never passes for him, there is no before and after, only one simultaneous 'now'. However, it can be argued that any action must take place in time and if an action happens in time (as a miracle clearly does), then the actor must also be in time. Nelson Pike in a comprehensive book *God and Timelessness* mounts a sustained attack on the view that a timeless God acts in any way. He gives the example of a 17,000-foot mountain which suddenly came into existence yesterday on the plains of Illinois. All the local believers point to this as an act of God. If, however, the mountain came into existence yesterday, surely this means that God acted yesterday as well? However if God is timeless he could not act *yesterday* since God is outside all time – indeed a timeless God could not act in time in any way. To even say that he could is a contradiction in terms.

On the face of it this argument is strong, but it is not as clearly right as it may first appear. It is important to remember that God who is timeless substance has all times equally present to him in one glorious 'now'. Assume, therefore, that there are a number of events which take place at times T1, T2, T3, T4 and T5 (which occur one after the other at whatever interval you like to imagine). It is possible to argue that the timeless God could timelessly will that all these events will take place at the stated times even though he himself is not in any of these times. All time would be present to this God and since this God knows past, present and future simultaneously, he could simultaneously will that all the events in the history of the universe (past, present and future) should take place in the order they appear to take place to us. In order to will this, God himself does not have to be in time.

The issue is not, therefore, clear-cut and the argument is keenly debated. It is not clear, however, that those who reject the idea of timeless action have proved their case and, in principle, it still seems possible to maintain that a timeless God could bring things about in time – *provided* you think that God as a timeless actor who knows things that happen in time makes sense at all. At the very least, a good deal of mystery is involved in this view; but this view of God depends on the idea that we really know nothing about what God is like in himself, and so the emphasis on mystery is appropriate. If you accept that a timeless God can act, then you can still maintain that miracles seen as violations of laws of nature can take place with God conceived as timeless substance or 'timeless pure act'. It is important, however, to recognise that those who do not share this view of God are likely to reject the idea of a timeless God acting in any way in a temporal universe.

Given, then, the first of the four ideas of miracle set out at the beginning of this chapter (i.e. a miracle as a breach of the laws of nature by an action of God), it would seem not unreasonable for someone who believes, on other grounds, in God defined *either* as an everlasting personal individual *or* (more arguably) as timeless substance also to believe in this form of miracle. If, however, you believe in God as an existing reality within the language of religious believers or consider talk of God to be affirming a particular way in which life can be lived, then this view of miracle must be rejected.

2 Miracle as an action by God which is not against laws of nature

The second type of miracle (an event seen as an act by God intervening in the world which does not, nevertheless, go against laws of nature) can again only be believed in by those who accept the view of God as personal and everlasting or as timeless substance. Since 'God' under the third and fourth views (as set out in ch. 3) cannot act, this view of miracle is not a possibility under these latter two views. However even though the possibility is open under the first two conceptions of God, there are still considerable problems which need to be recognised.

Imagine an example. A mother who believes in God (viewed as an everlasting, personal individual or timeless substance) prays for help for her daughter who is sitting an important examination. The results come through and the daughter has passed with really excellent marks. The mother claims that God has intervened to help her daughter. Another example might be a ship sinking in a typhoon. All the crew are reported drowned. The wife of one of the men prays and firmly believes that God has answered her prayer. She sets out alone to search for her husband and, after much effort, finds him marooned as the sole survivor living on an uninhabited island. She immediately claims a miracle. The problem in both these cases is that although the mother in the first case and the wife in the second may claim that a miracle has taken place, although they may firmly believe this, there is no evidence that any divine intervention has taken place. In the first example the daughter's tutor may have been expecting an excellent set of examination results and in the second case a series of coincidences could perfectly well explain the survival of the lone individual.

This category of miracle is, therefore, close to (3) below – it is a belief that can neither be proved or disproved. No evidence counts in favour or against the hypothesis. In any case, the mechanics in this type of situation are difficult to explain. Believers tend to want to make two claims which appear to be contradictory:

(a) on the one hand they claim that God is involved in all acts, i.e. in everything that happens; yet
(b) on the other hand they want to claim that some events are particularly brought about by God's action.

The separation of these two categories is by no means clear. There seem to be no objective grounds for claiming that an event falls under (b) above rather than (a) – it really rests on the opinion of the believer who considers that certain events are brought about by God and others are not. Almost everything, therefore, depends on how the individual regards a particular event. Nothing within the event itself will decide the issue.

Probably the most common situation in which this type of 'action by God' is claimed, is when a believer looks back over his or her life and claims God has 'guided' him or her in whatever the individual has done. When pressed, various crucial events may be pointed to, but the outsider can easily explain these as coincidences. The one person claims that God has acted, the second denies it. John Wisdom (in an article 'Gods' in A. Flew's (ed., *Logic and Language*, vol. 1) gives an excellent picture of this in his example of the invisible gardener:

Imagine that two people both come across a neglected garden. The first says that a gardener must have been there because he can see order and beauty, the way certain flowers are arranged and other features pointing to care and attention. The second, however, sees no such evidence.

He maintains that if there were a gardener there would be no weeds, the whole garden would be much tidier. Both individuals agree on the facts, but their interpretations differ. The individuals may sit up all night looking for the gardener, they may set up all sorts of tests to try to detect the gardener, but still the issue is not settled. The first individual claims that the gardener must be invisible and spiritual so that he is not detected by any test, the second simply says there is no gardener.

The parallel, of course, is with God and the world. Believer and non-believer do not differ on any facts about the world – they differ only in their interpretation. If, therefore, the believer claims a miracle while the non-believer merely sees the result of coincidence or the normal causal process at work within the world, the difference between the two is solely a matter of interpretation.

It follows, therefore, that this second view of miracle is open to anyone who believes, on other grounds, that God exists as defined in chapter 2 as an everlasting personal individual or as timeless substance (provided, in the latter case, he or she considers that such a God can act at all). No evidence will count for or against this hypothesis, but this does not mean that the hypothesis is irrational.

3 Miracle as an event or circumstance seen as having religious significance

On the surface, this view of miracle appears identical to (2) above, but this is not the case. Unlike (2), this approach to miracles does not require a God who is either an everlasting personal individual or timeless substance. Any event which a member of the believing community considers to have religious significance may be seen as a miracle. If, therefore, God's reality is seen to exist within the believing community, if 'God' is to be found wherever two or three gather together in his name then miracle can be found wherever the religious dimension in life is particularly apparent.

There may be many things that appear miraculous under this heading. The night sky on a clear night in the country may help an individual to see his or her true position in the universe, the sight may help the individual to reorder his or her priorities and to see that, in the light of the enduring reality of the universe, all the things that the individual has dedicated his or her life to are mistaken and, instead, a new approach to life is called for. The night sky may, thus, truly be seen as miraculous and the experience may mark a turning point in an individual's life away from selfishness and concern with the transitory things of this world and towards a new attitude to life which can provide meaning and fulfilment whatever happens. On this view, therefore, no 'Being, Spirit or individual' outside the universe is necessary. Believers in God seen as an everlasting, personal individual or as timeless substance can both believe in miracles as defined under this heading. They may well see particular events or circumstances as somehow being brought about by the God they believe in who is outside the universe as well as being intimately involved with it. Those who look on 'God' as a reality within religious language or consider that talk of God affirms a possible way in which life can be lived, can also believe in miracles as defined here. They will not see any 'Being, Spirit or individual' called God being involved as they reject such an idea. However the reality that they consider God to be can still be pointed to by miraculous events. These might be looked on almost as 'disclosure events' – events which disclose the reality that is God to the individual.

Under all four conceptions of God, what is regarded as a miracle under this heading will be what appears to be such by the individual. There is nothing within any particular event or circumstance that validates the claim to be a 'miracle' as here defined. What is important is the effect on the individual. The claim to be a miracle is, therefore, based on the way things are perceived. There is no way of separating:

– this is a miracle (defined as an event or circumstance having religious significance); and
– it appears to X that this is a miracle.

To the outsider who rejects all ideas of God, all possibilities of miracle will be rejected. He or she must still admit, however, that certain events or circumstances can transform an individual's life and can provide a turning point towards a totally different perspective. The rejection of miracle may be accepted, but at the least these events can be seen as remarkable.

4 Miracle as a transformation in a human life

There are two possible views of man. David Hume considered that a 'science of man' was possible. One way of putting this might be to say that if we knew enough about any person we could predict how they would act. Imagine that it was possible to know every detail about a man or woman – their precise genetic make-up, all the influences that affected the individual throughout his or her life and all the external affects on each person – then it would be possible to predict exactly how each individual would act in any circumstance. The Danish philosopher/theologian, Søren Kierkegaard, took quite the reverse stance in maintaining that each individual is autonomous and free, that each person is free to choose and free to act without being a product of their culture or background. These two views are, therefore, radically different.

In David Hume's view people are unlikely to surprise. A man or woman's actions are basically predictable and the only element of surprise arises if we do not know the individual in question well enough to be able to predict their reaction in any particular situation. Søren Kierkegaard's approach, however, claims that people can always surprise – any individual can act out of character. Every man or woman is, in the end, free and can act as a free individual in any situation.

If, therefore, Kierkegaard's view is taken it is possible that a moral transformation can occur at any time and this may be seen as a miracle. A hardened killer who has never shown compassion or any interest in any other person may suddenly show love, compassion and unselfishness when it is least expected. A businessman who has devoted his life to money and success may decide to abandon everything and to live with and care for the poor and needy in some distant area of the world.

Believers in God defined as personal and everlasting or as timeless substance could claim such a miracle as being due to the God they believe in. The believer who sees God's reality existing within the language of the believing community can affirm that miracles (as here defined) do indeed occur. A believer who relates his or her life to the reality that is God may indeed find his or her life transformed in a truly 'miraculous' and surprising way. Lastly those who see talk of God as affirming the possibility of a different way in which life can be lived, can claim that in each individual's life miraculous transformations are possible as the individual rejects the normally accepted order of priorities and instead sees the value of living life *sub specie aeternitatis*.

Supporters of all four views of 'God' can, therefore, all claim the possibility of this type of miracle.

5 Summary

To sum up, therefore, miracles can be seen in four ways:

(1) As a breach of a law of nature. Only believers in God defined as an everlasting, personal individual or timeless substance can believe in this type of miracle. In the case of believers in the latter idea of God, however, they must first decide whether a God so defined can act in any way at all. If they decide he can, then this view of miracle is a possibility.

(2) As an act by God intervening in the world in accordance with the known laws of nature. Again only believers in God defined as an everlasting individual or as timeless substance can believe in this option. Even if they do, this view of miracle is entirely dependent on the way an individual sees a particular event or circumstance.

(3) As a particular event or circumstance having religious significance. Believers in God defined in all four ways set out in chapter 3 can hold this view of miracle. As in the case of the second type of miracle above, it is again a highly subjective position.

(4) A miracle as a transformation which can take place within a human being. Again upholders of all four views of God

can affirm this possibility – provided they reject David Hume's idea of man and instead, with Kierkegaard, see man as being autonomous and free.

The attractions of the third and fourth views of miracles include the fact that miracles are not restricted to gaps in our scientific knowledge. The believers who want to maintain that miracles as defined in the first two ways above do occur, may well find themselves in difficulties in showing to the sceptic just why a particular event should be regarded as miraculous. In the end, there is probably no answer to the critic who says that any miracle could be explained if only we had sufficient scientific knowledge. However the individual who believes in God on other grounds can still reasonably maintain that miracles occur, even if he or she has to admit that they provide no ground for conversion of the non-believer.

5

Prayer

1 Why analyse prayer?

Believers pray. This is a common feature of all religions which believe in a God. Prayer can take many forms; it may be praying for forgiveness, praying for things to happen (petitionary prayer), giving thanks or simple prayer involving contemplation of God. Prayer sometimes involves language but this is not always the case. Sometimes the believer simply holds himself before God in an awareness of God's presence: the injunction to pray continuously may be the call to an individual to live his or her whole life as if it is a prayer – in other words, everything that is done and said in the individual's life is done and said as if in the presence of God. If religion is to retain any content of its own and is not to be reduced to morality or denied altogether, then a satisfactory account must be given of prayer.

It is one thing, however, to say that an account must be given of prayer and quite another to give such an account. Prayer lies at the heart of the spiritual life. Here, as in other areas, the conception of God that each individual works with will have a determining effect on what the individual considers is happening when he or she prays. Many believers dislike philosophy as they feel, instinctively, that when they look closely and hard at prayer, this in itself will make prayer more difficult and possibly destroy it altogether. As soon as the believer stops to analyse prayer, its reality may be destroyed. In a way it is like love. Imagine a young couple who are in love: if one of them stops to analyse closely just *why* he or she is in love, they may find the relationship spoilt. What was previously accepted and enjoyed, and which provided the pivot around which each individual's life turned, becomes soured and somehow debased once it is questioned and analysed. This can also happen with prayer. Having said this, however, there are various reasons why it is important to consider what *is* happening when the believer prays (most of these reasons apply equally to other areas of religious belief as well):

(a) The believer who takes his or her religion seriously will wish to communicate this to others and, in order to do this, the believer himself needs to be clear on what is involved. It is no good saying to a questioning young person, 'Do this, but I don't know what is happening or what you should expect when you do it'. Many young people are turned away from religion by just this sort of vagueness. Some degree of clarity is required.

(b) Believers themselves, when they pray, will be unable to prevent asking themselves at times just what their prayers are meant to achieve – if, indeed, they consider that talk of 'achievement' is appropriate in relation to prayer (conversation, after all, does not have any particular 'achievement' as an objective). What is the purpose of prayer? A believer who never even has to ask this question is either very secure indeed in the faith professed or is not taking prayer seriously.

(c) All believers will experience prayers which do not appear to be answered and they need to give some account of this experience if prayer is to retain its meaning and value.

When considering what prayer involves, God needs to be the starting point for any discussion as so much depends on what God is.

2 Praying to God seen as an everlasting individual

In many ways the simplest way of explaining prayer is to see it as part of a dialogue between the believer and an everlasting, personal God. Prayer can be looked at as part of a two-way relationship between individuals. The individual addresses God as 'Thou', as if addressing a person. Normal language is used and the words mean what they appear to mean. In petitionary prayer at least the believer is asking God for help and expects this help to materialise. The person praying does not believe that his or her prayers can be used to manipulate God, but he or she does believe that God hears the prayers and can respond if he chooses to do so. This response is not simply a matter of a change being brought about in the individual (see sections 4 and 5 below), but of God (who exists as an individual apart from the universe although closely involved with), intervening in some spiritual and supernatural manner in the world.

The majority of Christian believers consider that this is what prayer involves. They recognise that not all prayers will be answered and, indeed, that 'God knows best'. It is for this reason that they consider Jesus taught them to pray, 'Thy will be done'. In this prayer they recognise that although the individual may make requests to God, God knows far more about every situation than they do and his decision must, in the end, be final. If some prayers are unanswered then the believer trusts, by faith, in God and even though the actual outcome may go against what has been prayed for, he or she will still maintain that the prayers have been heard but that, for some good reason, God has decided to act in an alternative manner.

This comparatively straightforward account, however, suffers from considerable difficulties including:

(a) God is held to be OMNISCIENT (i.e. he knows everything), to be OMNIPOTENT (i.e. he can do anything) and he is wholly good. We shall discuss the precise meaning of these terms in chapter 7. But if God knows everything and is wholly good, why should a believer have to pray? Surely if God knows what a believer needs and if he is wholly good and omnipotent, he will ensure that the believer's needs are catered for? On this basis, therefore, prayer seems unnecessary.

(b) If God is omniscient, omnipotent and wholly good, surely he will bring about whatever is necessary for everyone? To conceive of a God who will ignore the needs of human beings simply because they do not pray for themselves and no one else prays for them seems to reduce the idea of God's goodness and compassion very considerably indeed and instead to substitute an idea of a God who will only cater for the needs of his followers if they abase themselves before him.

(c) Jesus told his followers that whatever they asked in faith they would receive and said that faith could move mountains. How, then, does one explain the death of a child from starvation when his father prays desperately for food? Surely it is inadequate to say that the father did not pray hard enough; that he was not good enough or that he was not a good Anglican, Baptist, Catholic, Methodist, Quaker, etc. Similarly, many would maintain that it is not adequate to say that the child's death was allowed by God in order to assist in the development of the father's 'soul'.

(d) If God does answer prayer in a straightforward manner, it should be possible to prepare a statistical analysis of, for instance, the rate of recovery from cancer of patients who have been prayed for and those who have not. In other words there should be *some* evidence that prayer does, indeed, make a difference. There is, however, no such evidence. If the believer replies to this by saying, 'Ah, God answers prayers in ways that the believer does not expect', then what can one make of this? If I ask an individual for X and instead Y happens, is this an answer? Also the believer may not be able to explain why Y might not have happened in any case and when he or she claims that Y is an 'answer to prayer' the individual may just be describing events that would have occurred in any case in terms that are congenial to the believer.

(e) When considering prayer for forgiveness, does not the idea of praying in this way to an everlasting individual imply the idea of God as a great judge who will condemn us after death if we do not say 'Sorry' to him for sins we have committed before we die? If God *is* conceived in this way, then can he any longer be looked on as loving and compassionate? (Some believers might reply to this by saying that the idea of God as loving has been overdone in recent years. The Bible does indeed affirm that God is a loving father, but the element of the 'fear of God' is also present and this aspect is often neglected today. It is this side of God which would give content to the idea of God as judge.)

(f) The mechanics of God intervening or acting in the world are far from clear. Does the believer in a God conceived in these terms see him as a continual 'tinkerer', i.e. as someone who continually intervenes in the universe to alter states of affairs that would have been otherwise except for the prayers of the faithful? In other words, if the believer thinks that God acts in response to prayer, it would appear that God is continuously active in the universe. In some way God changes the outcome of events and actions based on the prayers of believers. This idea of God continually intervening in the world can seem to reduce man's freedom and raises problems with separating those events which are the results of the natural course of events alone and those which are due to some 'special action' by God.

It must be admitted that these are very considerable difficulties and clear answers to them are far from easy (if, indeed, they are available at all). Most of these issues cannot be adequately dealt with by philosophers, although many attempts have been made and opinions vary as to their explanatory power. We do not have space to explore these problems, but the believer will have to resort to claims to 'faith' and 'trust' at a fairly early stage in the discussion. The attempts that have been made to overcome the difficulties (e.g. by Vincent Brummer in *What Are We Doing When We Pray?* (SCM 1984)) leave many unanswered questions. Outsiders to the particular belief system are unlikely to find answers that they would consider philosophically satisfying, and many believers do not feel the need for such answers. As the prophet Habbakuk says, 'The righteous shall live by his faith' (Habbakuk 2:4). In other words, the believer will live in trust and reliance on God. Even though he or she may recognise the problems, these will not affect his or her belief in or relationship with God.

These philosophic difficulties, however, are part of the reason why alternative accounts of prayer (such as those set out under sections (4) and (5) below) are increasingly accepted by sophisticated believers – even those who conceive of God as everlasting and personal.

It is probably fair to say that any account of prayer under this conception of God is going to have to be accepted 'like a little child' and philosophic analysis will not clear the muddy waters. The alternatives may be, therefore, between accepting prayer with a childlike faith (in spite of the factors mentioned in (1) above) and a philosophic analysis which is likely to favour one of the alternative accounts of prayer set out under (4) and (5) below, even if these views are combined with a view of God as everlasting and apart from the world but who is, nevertheless, not seen as continuously active in the universe. In other words an everlasting, individual God who does not intervene but allows laws of nature to take their normal course.

3 Prayer seen as addressing God conceived as timeless substance

In a similar way to the conception of God as an everlasting individual, God conceived as timeless substance or pure act (ch. 3, section 2) is in some mysterious sense 'out there' – transcendent and yet immanent in creation. However, there are considerable differences. When God is conceived as literally timeless, things which appear as past, present or future in the universe are all equally present to God. God, therefore, knows timelessly what every individual will pray at every single moment in his or her life. God knows what you will pray on your death bed and the prayer that you will then make is just as present to God as the creation of the universe or some event that will occur in ten million years time. In prayer, therefore, the believer is certainly not telling God anything since he knows everything, absolutely in the past, present and future in one single all-embracing 'now'. Prayer in this view of God is not so much part of a two-way relationship (as it is under the everlasting view of God above) since relationships occur in time and God is outside time. Having said this, advocates of this view can still affirm (as we shall see) that God knows what the believer prays and takes this into account.

There are three central problems relating to prayer when God is seen as literally timeless:

(a) Since God knows everything absolutely, including what will happen at every moment in the history of the universe and since God timelessly knows what the believer is going to pray, what is the believer doing when he or she prays?
(b) If God knows what everyone will pray and will do in the future, are we free to choose whether or not to pray? If God knows our future actions, are we not rather like totally predictable puppets? and
(c) Can a timeless God act at all in response to prayer? (See chapter 4(1) for a brief discussion as to whether it makes sense to talk of a timeless God 'acting' in time.)

It is the first two of the above which raise the major issues that we need to focus on in order to be clear on how prayer is to be regarded under this view of God.

Aquinas gave a helpful picture of the timeless God's relationship to time; he asks us to imagine that time is stretched out like a road going backwards from where we are now and forwards to the future. God is rather like an observer on a very high mountain looking down at the road and seeing all points on the road simultaneously but not himself being on the road. Aquinas says: 'He who walks on a road does not see those who come after him, but he who looks at the road from some height sees all at once those who are walking on the road' (*Summa Theologiae* 1.14.13).

God, therefore, sees everything that happens on the 'road of time' simultaneously. This is a useful picture (although I shall argue later in this section that it may not be an adequate one) and can assist with an analysis of prayer. If we imagine various points in an individual's life which are stretched out on the road of time, these points can be named T1, T2, T3, T4 and T5 where 'T' stands for time and 1, 2, 3, 4 and 5 are different points in time. Assume that you were born at T1 and the moment of your death is T5. The time is now T3 and next week will be T4. God knows what you will pray at T4 and T5 and he knows this timelessly (as he is looking down as if from the mountain and seeing all points on the road of time simultaneously).

As God timelessly knows what you will pray at T4 and T5, he can timelessly decide to answer your prayer. He will timelessly decide to take into account what he knows you are going to pray next week at T4 (T4 is, of course, in the future so far as you are concerned but it is not future to God since, as God is timeless, there is no past or future to him). Prayer can, thus, have an effect on God since, if God knows (timelessly) that you were not going to pray in a certain way at T4, he would not have brought certain things about following your prayer. God, according to this view, has the whole of the universe's history stretched out simultaneously before him, and he has timelessly decided (in one single instant, as it were) how everything will happen.

On this view, therefore, a relationship can be seen between what the believer prays for and the results of the prayer. It can even make sense for the believer to pray for things that have happened in the past, since God timelessly knows what you will pray and could, therefore, take into account at T2 the prayer uttered at T3. However, this does not explain why God answers some prayers and not others nor in exactly what way prayer is answered (the problems outlined in (2) above continue, therefore, to apply under this heading as well).

We now have to tackle the second of the three problems listed above – namely, if God knows timelessly what you will pray at T4 (next week) and at T5 (on your death bed), are you free? This problem was addressed by Boethius. Boethius was a remarkable figure – a Consul of ancient Rome, he was imprisoned by his enemies and saw a virtuous life very badly rewarded indeed. He wrote a book in prison called the *Consolation of Philosophy* (which is easy to read and enjoyable), in which he holds a conversation with the 'Lady Philosophy'. The book is a dialogue between Boethius and this imaginary lady representing the truths that philosophy seeks. Boethius deals with many and varied issues, such as why good men are so often badly treated. However, one of the chief problems he considers is whether we can be free if God knows the future. Boethius's argument is also used, in different forms, by St Augustine, St Anselm and St Thomas Aquinas, so the pedigree is excellent!

The Lady Philosophy argues with Boethius that God's knowledge of our future free actions does not mean that we are not free. Imagine that there was no God at all, then there would be no problem in asserting that individuals are free. If, now, God is introduced who knows what our future free choices will be, this does not take away human freedom. God is timeless so all time is equally present to him. He therefore knows what our choices will be: we cannot, therefore, surprise him; he cannot be proved wrong. He knows exactly what we and every other individual on earth will pray in what to us is the future, but this does not mean that he forces or coerces people to pray in a certain way; they are free to choose, but whatever choice they make he will know the result of the choice.

It is possible, therefore, on this view to maintain that God (seen as timeless substance) knows everything that will occur and yet this does not restrict human freedom and, further, to maintain that God can act in response to prayer (*provided* it is considered reasonable to say that a timeless God can act at all – and this, as we saw in chapter 4, is a much debated issue). In prayer, according to this view, the believer can see himself as praying and God timelessly knows what this prayer will be. Whether the believer chooses to pray or not and however the prayer is framed, God will still know and he can timelessly decide whether and how to act in response.

Although I have used Aquinas' example of God looking down on the road of time from a timeless mountain, it is not, perhaps, a good example, at least if taken literally. It is an attempt to place God, as it were, in another dimension. Human life is seen as being two-dimensional on the road of time whilst God, in the third dimension, can look down on our two-dimensional life. This picture, however, does not work. We are familiar with three dimensions and possibly time itself as a fourth dimension. But if God is somehow in another dimension of which we are not aware, this cannot negate the previous dimensions. A fourth dimension does not rule out the other three, so if God is on the mountain this does not mean that the first two dimensions would not apply to him. Similarly it is difficult to see how time does not pass for God and how God can be timelessly said to know things and to act. Having said this, I recognise that Aquinas might say that I am guilty of taking the example too literally. As we have seen previously, talk of God as timeless substance is largely restricted to metaphorical talk. It is literally true that God is timeless, but almost everything else we can know about him is metaphorical. This metaphorical language may be true and helpful, but it must not be taken literally. By taking it literally, I am reducing the mystery that is God to something that can be understood by humans and this (Aquinas would hold) must not and cannot be done.

It is, therefore, important to realise that in all discussions of God under this option, mystery and 'picture' language is going to be central. This is not to devalue 'picture' language which may still be true; the picture may convey a truth about God to man in the only way that this truth can be shown. God is 'other' than us, and we can not use human language to refer literally, 'univocally' (see chapter 3 (2)), to God except in a very restricted sense. In prayer, the believer is expressing his or her wishes before whatever God is and holding him or herself open to whatever God wants for us. We cannot know what action (if any) we can expect from God in response to our prayers, since we do not know what it is for God to act.

4 Prayer to the existing reality of God found within religious language

D. Z. Phillips, in *The Concept of Prayer*, gives a comprehensive picture of prayer when God is viewed as a reality within religious language. Phillips deals with all forms of Christian prayer and it is easy to read his book and to feel that he has, indeed, covered Christian prayer fully and fairly, thus expressing the essence of prayer. On closer examination, however, this is not so clearly the case.

Phillips maintains that prayer does not change God (in this he endorses one of the strands held by those who see God as timeless substance) but rather that it changes the person who utters the prayer. God does not come to know anything when an individual tells him of his or her sins. Prayer derives its meaning from the content in which it is uttered and one can measure whether prayer is genuine or not by seeing the role it plays in the life of the believer. This view takes seriously the connection between prayer and the rest of life. Prayer is only possible in a life orientated towards God. A prayer uttered in a moment of crisis by someone who has not participated in religious belief is not, in this view, genuine prayer at all. Prayer requires devotion, and we can recognise whether prayer is genuine by seeing the role that prayer plays in an individual's life. (There are clear echoes here of Wittgenstein's position set out in chapter 3 (section 3) that the meaning of religious language is to be found by looking at the role language, including the language of prayer, plays in believers' lives.) Prayer is primarily a matter of coming to self-knowledge and also of finding meaning and hope in life whatever happens.

In the case of petitionary prayer (for instance praying for things such as the cure of someone who has a disease, for help in some situation that the believer faces or for war to be stopped), Phillips rejects totally the idea that this is talking to a God 'out there'. Instead he maintains that the heart of all Christian prayer is the phrase that Jesus used in Gethsemane, 'Thy will be done', or the phrase in the prayer that Jesus taught his disciples, 'Thy will be done on earth as it is in Heaven'. In both these prayers the believer is bringing him or herself to face whatever will be the case. In other words these prayers are an attempt by the believer to relate him or herself to the reality of God found within the believing community and within religious language and, by so doing, to find the strength to face whatever will happen in life. Petitionary prayer is *not*, therefore, asking for God outside the universe to in some way intervene to provide supernatural help. Petitionary prayer is always valid provided it is part of a religious life (this is a considerable strength as there are no problems of 'unanswered prayer' to deal with).

According to this view, if a mother prays for her child who is dying of leukemia, what she is really doing, if she is not superstitious, is simply meditating in such a way that she can bring herself to face whatever the outcome of the disease may be. Specifically she is *not* praying for a miracle as an action by God against (or even in conformity with) the natural order – Phillips maintains that anyone who considers that this is what believers are asking for when they pray is very superstitious.

Prayer is, thus, a matter of an individual coming to self-knowledge or a ritual whose purpose lies in itself. Prayer is not a substitute for effort but a way for the individual to better understand where his or her effort should best be directed. When an individual goes to church, he or she goes apart from the world and orders his or her thoughts so as to guide future actions. He or she will come out of the service feeling renewed and with a clearer direction and purpose in life. The idea of prayer as a form of ritual whose value lies in itself has considerable merit. Many church services are repetitive; believers make the same prayers week after week and some believers do not look on these prayers as being part of a 'two-way relationship' (as suggested by the view of God as an everlasting individual). To see church services as an opportunity for quiet reflection and meditation which results in inner renewal is a cogent view.

One problem with the linguistic view of prayer (at least in so far as it is intended, as it is, to represent what Christianity affirms) is that Jesus was, on its own terms, very superstitious indeed. Christians have traditionally affirmed that prayer *does* make a difference and this difference is not just a difference to the believer. If one goes into almost any Christian church when a service is taking place, the believers there are making requests to God which are based on the assumption that God (and a God who is in some sense 'out there') can and does intervene in the world. In other words, most believers reject the linguistic view of petitionary prayer. However this does not necessarily mean that they are right to do so – often, the more sophisticated believers are, the more they are willing to see prayer in this form. This may well be because they recognise just how difficult it is to give a satisfactory account of prayer in traditional terms (as we saw in section 2 above).

5 Prayer when talk of God affirms a different way of living life

In chapter 3 (section 4), Stewart Sutherland's example was given of Jesus in the Garden of Gethsemane. In praying on the eve of his crucifixion, Jesus (says Sutherland) is considering the alternatives available to him on the morrow. Does he remain true to himself and therefore suffer a terrible death or does he avoid this, avoid the fate that awaits him (as he clearly could have done) and thus fail to remain true to what he had taught and believed throughout his life? Jesus prays and in his prayer asks himself these questions. He relates his life to the alternative way of living that he had affirmed throughout his ministry. His life had been grounded in the eternal – he had lived life *sub specie aeternitatis* and had rejected all the things that the world considered important – money, family, home, comfort and security. He could escape the fate that awaited him, but he knew that, if he did so, he would betray all that mattered most to him. He would lose his own integrity.

In prayer, therefore, the believer is attempting to see his life from a different perspective. He (or she) is asking himself whether his life has conformed with the possible way of life he has sought to live. In the film *Goodbye Mr Chips*, the theme song has a verse:

In the evening of my life I will turn to the sunset,
At a moment in my day, when my life is through,
And the question I will ask only I can answer –
Was I brave, and strong and true?
Did I fill the world with love my whole life through?

In other words only the individual can ask himself the question, and only he or she can provide the answer, as to whether his or her life has lived up to the possible way in which life could be lived. Praying for forgiveness, according to this view, is asking yourself whether you have lived as you should have done and deciding to turn round your actions in the future to live in the way that you know is right. It is a matter of coming to terms with past failures and being able to live with yourself when you recognise how far you have fallen short of the ideal. Similarly, when looking to the future, the individual is trying to see the right way forward and, by bringing himself or herself into touch with the reality which is affirmed by talking about God (see ch. 3 (4)), is seeking the right way forward in life – just as Sutherland suggests Jesus was doing in the Garden of Gethsemane.

Salvation, according to this view, is a matter of human wholeness, of coming to terms with past failures and literally being saved from the adverse effects of sin on each individual. Aristotle maintained that at first all men are free, but as each individual does good or bad actions, so future similar actions become easier and easier. In other words a man becomes virtuous or vicious by leading a virtuous or vicious life. Doing evil things is, therefore, to live on a slippery slope – each evil action makes future evil actions easier. Sin drags us down. According to this view, praying for forgiveness is the attempt to turn ourselves round towards the good, and we seek salvation in this life by saving ourselves from the results of our past failures. Relating oneself to 'God' is, therefore, a way of saving ourselves from our sins by attempting to turn ourselves round to the possible way of living life that is open to everyone.

This view, therefore, sees a value and a purpose in prayer. The individual is taking time apart from the world to reorder his or her priorities, to see how life so far has measured up to the ideal and to consider the future. To be religious is to see that there is a different possible way in which life can be lived, to see that life does not have to be trivialised by the passage of the years and the frustration of human endeavours, to see that each and every human being has a value and can be grounded in the eternal ('the eternal', it must be remembered, does not represent some heavenly realm after death but rather a different way of living this life). To be grounded like this, however, requires commitment and dedication, it requires effort and sacrifice, and in prayer the believer is keeping himself 'on track' towards his objective.

In a similar way, in prayer the individual recognises his or her own wants and desires before God. By bringing what matters most to an individual before the reality that is God (representing not an individual apart from the world but a different way in which life can be lived), the individual comes to see these requests in perspective. The dedicated believer will come to understand that asking in prayer for more money, a bigger car or material success is a confusion of objectives. These are not the sort of things that the reality that is God stands for. If these are uppermost in the believer's mind when he or she prays, the individual should come to see that his or her desires are misplaced. The individual who prays for these types of things is still living in the ordinary world and has not grounded himself in the way of living life represented by the Eternal. He or she is serving mammon and not God.

It is important to emphasise once again (see ch. 3, (4)) that this alternative way of living life is not a matter of personal choice or whim. The way of living life that the individual is trying to relate to is real, it exists. If it did not, then someone who sincerely chose the path of self-renunciation, of self-denial, someone who took the straight and narrow way would not be a saint but a madman. If anyone seriously tries to live the life of a saint rather than to be concerned with his own pleasure then this is, indeed, ridiculous unless this way of life is a real and existent possibility.

Prayer, thus, has a meaning, but it is not talking to some 'God' who is 'out there'. There is no such God under this view and the idea of a God 'out there' does not make sense. Prayer, however, retains its value. Much the same can be said if God is an existent reality within the language of religious believers.

6 Summary

If God is either a reality within the language of the believing community or if talk of God is affirming a different way in which life can be lived then prayer still has a value. Praying for forgiveness in both cases is a matter of turning round one's will in order to find release from past sins in a 'salvation' that lies in this life rather than beyond the grave. Petitionary prayer focuses on 'Thy will be done' and coming to accept whatever will be the case or in trying to relate one's life to the real possibility of a life lived *sub specie aeternitatis*. These views concentrate on the meditative effects of prayer on the individual.

If God is an everlasting individual, then prayer can be seen as a dialogue with God, as part of a two-way relationship between two individuals. Normal language is used and this retains its normal meaning. The believer prays in the expectation that God can and does answer prayers by intervening in the world. Praying for forgiveness is praying for the individual God, conceived as a judge, to forgive the believer for sins committed. However there are considerable philosophic difficulties with this account which cannot be easily resolved and, therefore, this view of prayer demands an almost child-like faith and trust.

If God is timeless substance, the philosophic difficulties that accompany the idea of God seen as an everlasting individual still remain. God, however, knows timelessly what everyone will pray in the future and has timelessly decided whether and how to answer the prayer. This knowledge by God of the individual's future actions is held not to limit the individual's freedom. The credibility of this view rests on acceptance of the idea that a timeless God can act and also on the fact that God is wholly other than us and very mysterious. The believer cannot, therefore, know what it means for God to 'act'.

It would, of course, be wrong to maintain that the medi-tative and therapeutic effects of prayer are rejected by those who see God as an everlasting individual or as timeless sub-stance. Meditation clearly does have an important part to play in prayer and the believer is certainly trying to turn his or her will round to conform with God's will. However those who see God as in some sense independent of the universe he has created maintain that there is more to it than that.

6

Eternal Life

1 What is eternal life?

Christianity has traditionally claimed that Christ came to bring eternal life to those who followed him. However 'eternal life' can mean various things. The major options are as follows:

(a) Eternal life as everlasting life after death for the individual in a heavenly kingdom which is social and where interaction takes place between those who have survived death and have arrived in this kingdom (rather than going elsewhere). There they dwell in the presence of God in a kingdom of enduring peace. This is, therefore, an idea of heaven as social and, after death, the believer considers that he or she will form part of a heavenly society.

(b) 'Eternal life' as life after death for the individual in which each individual enjoys the 'beatific vision' of God. The beatific vision is timeless and never changes. It is wholly satisfying and is the final end for man. Different people will experience the beatific vision in different ways, but in whatever way it is experienced it will be completely fulfilling. The vision is comprehensive and never alters (it cannot, of course, do so as any alteration would involve time and the beatific vision as well as the individual who experiences it is literally timeless, i.e. strictly outside time).

In chapter 2 the influence that Plato had on the formulation of the idea of God as timeless was outlined. Plato's influence continued in the formulation of the idea of the beatific vision. In the final chapter of Plato's *Symposium* there is a marvellous speech praising absolute, eternal beauty which Plato has Socrates retell. The speech praises in poetic form the absolute value of the contemplation of this unchangeable beauty and sees this as the highest of all ends for man. It is important to remember that Plato was thinking that Beauty was one of the Forms (see ch. 2). Plato is not thinking, therefore, of man looking at beautiful objects, beautiful ideas or even the beauty of God but rather at beauty itself. It can, of course, be asked whether it makes sense to talk in these terms of 'beauty' by itself. It is one thing to use beauty as an adjective to describe things, it is quite another to talk of contemplating beauty alone.

The early Church, having committed itself to a timeless God, also saw the attractions of the unchanging contemplation of God as the final end for man. There would then be no question of any progress after death to some higher end. Effectively, therefore, the Platonic forms of Beauty, Truth, Justice, Goodness, etc. were all seen as united in God. When, therefore, the individual attains the beatific vision of God, he or she also contemplates absolute Beauty, Truth, Goodness, etc.

It is important to remember that this is a view of a timeless and totally unchanging end for man – in marked contrast to the alternative position given in the paragraph above.

(c) 'Eternal life' as a different quality of this life. Thus in John 17:2 Jesus says: 'Father, the hour has come; glorify thy Son that the Son may glorify thee, since thou hast given him power over all flesh, to give eternal life to all whom thou hast given him. And this is eternal life, that they know thee the only true God and Jesus Christ whom thou has sent.' Again, Jesus says (in John 6:47): 'Truly, truly, I say unto you, he who believes has eternal life.'

In other words, the believer who comes to know God in this life will thereby come to live a different type of life and will thus experience eternal life. Eternal life, in this view, is not a life after death but an altered quality of life here and now.

The Church of England's Alternative Services Book published in 1980 changed the wording of the absolution from that in the Book of Common Prayer to concentrate on this idea of eternal life here and now. The Book of Common Prayer said: 'Almighty God ... have mercy upon you; pardon and deliver you from all your sins, confirm and strengthen you in all goodness, and *bring you to everlasting life* ...' The Alternative Service Book changes this to: 'Almighty God ... have mercy upon you, pardon and deliver you from all your sins, confirm and strengthen you in all goodness, and *keep you in life eternal.*' The emphasis has thus been altered – eternal life in the Alternative Service Book is seen as 'here and now' rather than 'to come'. Neither version rules out the other, but the priorities have been changed.

Many believers who have not seriously considered the issues combine the idea of a timeless beatific vision and an everlasting heavenly society. This is a position which is almost impossible to justify. *Either* heaven is a social kingdom in which time passes *or* the individual experiences the timeless beatific vision; the two cannot be brought together without modification. Life after death cannot be both outside time and within time simultaneously. This is a simple matter of logic. If 'timeless' is to be taken literally (which, as we have seen, Plato, Augustine, Boethius, Aquinas and many Catholic theologians considered that it was), then there is a straightforward choice to be made.

Aquinas maintained that, on death, the individual can suffer one of three possible fates. He or she will be judged immediately, as an individual, in the 'particular judgement' (this is the first of two judgements – the second, the 'general judgement' takes place when the world is brought to an end and when those who are living at that time as well as those who have died are judged together). At the particular judgement, the individual will face one of the three following possibilities:

(a) Be consigned to hell. Hell is everlasting (not timeless), as the pains that have to be endured in hell are so great that the human body could not stand them if their intensity was to be at the level required. The punishment is, therefore, extended for an everlasting time, i.e. it continues for ever and ever and ever.

(b) Pass to purgatory. Purgatory is the place where sins which have not been forgiven or where those sins that have been forgiven are, as required, expurgated by means of appropriate punishments. Purgatory is in time, but the intense pains which individual souls suffer in purgatory is eased by the knowledge that everyone in purgatory will eventually pass to the third possibility which some may go to directly on death.

(c) The timeless beatific vision.

Aquinas' view of the fate of the individual on death is still widely accepted within the Roman Catholic tradition, although it is rare to have the alternatives spelt out as clearly as Aquinas himself did. Possibly this may be because the idea of a heavenly society is much more appealing to the normal believer who hopes to meet again after death friends and relatives who have died. With the timeless beatific vision, this idea is not credible.

The existence of hell tends to be played down by many modern theologians and, indeed, many would question whether there is such a place or whether anyone (or at least more than a handful) ever go to hell. Various suggestions have been made to support this view including the idea that everyone is forgiven by God; that God in his mercy would never allow anyone to be permanently separated from him; that only those who actually choose to go to hell will go there or that in the last seconds of every individual's life he or she repents and therefore avoids permanent exile from God. These ideas may or may not be plausible, but they have restricted biblical support and, in the end, rest on a willingness to see the language of the Bible as metaphorical rather than in any sense literal.

The Westminster Confession of 1647 (the Presbyterian Confession of Faith) combines *both* the beatific vision and the idea of the heavenly kingdom in a form which makes sense and can be intellectually defended. It maintains that the beatific vision of God is an experience of the disembodied soul between death and the last day (i.e. the final day when

Christ will return and the world order will be brought to an end). Christ's return will herald the new kingdom of God which will be a social kingdom where, as Isaiah says: 'The wolf shall dwell with the lamb, and the leopard shall lie down with the kid, and the calf and the lion and the fatling together, and a little child shall lead them' (Isa. 11:6).

2 Which views of eternal life are tenable?

In section 1 above, three possible views of 'eternal life' were set out. Which views are tenable is going to depend directly on the definition of 'God' that you are operating with and here again, therefore, we come back to the four views of 'God' set out in chapter 3.

If you maintain that God is an everlasting, personal individual, then eternal life can be not only a different quality of this life but also life in a social heavenly kingdom after death. Existence after death can be claimed for each individual through the action of God (see the computer example in (3) below). The beatific vision could then be seen not as timeless vision which never changes, but rather as part of life in a heavenly kingdom in which God is known as an ever-present individual. God's glory would then fill this heaven, and the perception of this glory without end would be the everlasting equivalent to the timeless idea of the beatific vision.

The alternative view is to maintain that God is timeless substance. According to this view, a literally timeless heaven is more likely, with no idea of a heavenly society. Each individual who survives death and experiences this vision would then be timeless as well – in other words time would never pass. There could be no change, no interaction or relationships with other people (since these involve time) and, in short, it would be a fairly restricted idea of 'life' since life, as we know and experience it, involves time. The view taken of hell (which, as we have seen, Aquinas considered to be everlasting) could be either everlasting or timeless or, of course, the option is available for the believer to deny the existence of hell altogether. Certainly 'hell' as a concept is not popular in theological circles these days and many prefer to talk of 'alienation from God'. Whatever language is used, however, the existing individual who will experience this state will be either timeless or everlasting.

Both the above views can be combined with the idea of eternal life as a different quality of life here and now. In other words, this different quality of life commences now but will continue after death. So, to summarise so far, eternal life can be a different quality of life here and now combined with a life after death which is either timeless or everlasting. Which option is taken will probably depend on your view of God.

If your view of God is as a reality within religious language or if you join with those who consider that talk of God is affirming a different way in which life would be lived, then you are likely to be much more agnostic about life after death. The absence of a God 'out there' does not necessarily rule out life after death, but it does make it much less likely – particularly because of the problems of personal identity before and after death (see (3) below). On this view, it is more probable that the only sort of eternal life that an individual will experience is a different quality of life here and now. This has certainly been a strand in Christianity and has, perhaps, been too long neglected.

D. Z. Phillips' book *Death and Immortality* spells out the consequences of this view in some depth. He maintains that to 'live in the eternal' is to live your life in such a way that it is not vulnerable to contingencies or the way things turn out. Just as Socrates considered that the good man cannot be harmed, so the person for whom 'God' (defined as existing within the language of the believing community) is a reality in their life, cannot find life trivialised by the changes and chances of this fleeting world. Provided the individual has changed the orientation of his life so that he is relating his life to the good, provided he is always acting ethically and doing what is ethically good, then all that that individual undertakes in his life cannot be trivialised if his endeavours fail. What matters is the ethical decision, the fact that in everything the individual does, he is trying to do good. If his efforts are not crowned with success, if the individual's honesty means that he does not get promotion at work or if he will not compromise his principles, then provided this is the most important thing in his life nothing can take this away. In this way (advocates of this view maintain) the individual can never be separated from the 'love of God'.

Critics of the linguistic view might maintain that, although Christianity has indeed considered that the Christian experiences a different quality of life here and now, it also insists that the individual's life will continue after death. Thus Jesus says in John 6:54: ' . . . he who eats my flesh and drinks my blood has eternal life, and I will raise him up at the last day.' The first half of this verse could be seen to support the linguistic philosophers' view, but the second half is equally important and this the linguistic philosopher must deny.

It is important to remember that the linguistic view of God is *not* of some everlasting personal individual or timeless substance. God is either a reality within religious language – a reality which can be of supreme value for the individual and which he or she may be willing to give his or her life for (like other realities such as 'loyalty to country') – or talk about God affirms a possible way in which life can be lived. According to the latter view, 'eternal life' represents this alternative way of life.

Stewart Sutherland, in *God, Jesus and Belief* (pp. 83–6), has a good example. In Robert Bolt's play *A Man for All Seasons*, Thomas More is portrayed as talking to the ambitious young man, Rich, who has come to More for a position in order to seek power and advancement. More sees what Rich wants and recognises that Rich is planning to base his life on a mistake – on the search for power and glory. He suggests to Rich that he should become a teacher and says that, if he does so and if he is a good teacher, then: 'You will know it, your pupils will know it and God will know it.' However, for Sutherland, 'God will know it' does not mean that some entity somewhere beyond the sky will know about it. Rather, More is trying to show Rich that it is possible for him to live his life in a totally different and more worthwhile way than Rich is at present contemplating. Instead of seeking power, fortune and reputation, Rich could dedicate himself to the service of others and, in so doing, he would find 'eternal life' as a different quality of life here and now. Effectively, Sutherland argues, Jesus and Socrates were making the same point – that a different way of living life is available to each and every individual.

Sutherland's view is sophisticated and philosophically plausible, but it omits (as do the views of the linguistic philosophers) the fact that Jesus, Socrates and Thomas More all believed in a life after death and, when they talked of God, were not just talking of a different way of living life. Perhaps they were wrong to think of God in the terms they did, but there is little doubt that their conceptions of God went much beyond Sutherland's. There is here an important difference between Phillips as an exponent of view 3 and Sutherland of view 4. Phillips maintains that the linguistic idea of God affirms what believers actually believe. In this, at least, he is wrong. Believers do not think in these terms; they actually think that God is in some sense capable of love and of interaction with the world and exists apart from the universe that he has created. Sutherland, by contrast, is suggesting a revisionary account – a way in which Christian ideas can be reinterpreted for the next century. His views may not be traditional, but they have great depth and many advantages and he does at least recognise that he is engaged on a revisionary exercise and is not giving a description of what believers actually believe.

Having reviewed the alternative meanings of 'eternal life', it is necessary to consider, at least briefly, what it is that survives death. This will only be relevant to the extent that 'eternal life' involves the individual's survival of death which, as explained above, is not necessarily the case. If, however, someone believes in God defined as an everlasting individual or as timeless substance and also believes that the individual survives death and will enjoy eternal life (either as everlasting or timeless) after death, then whether it makes sense to say that 'I' survive is clearly an important issue.

3 What survives death?

Assuming that an individual survives death, what is it that survives? The person's body is clearly dead and buried or cremated – it has ceased to exist. How, then, can one meaningfully talk of the individual living on? Much depends on what a human person is considered to be. There are three main possibilities:

(a) A person is made up of mind and body. These are separate but they interact. On death, the body dies but the 'soul' or mind (which is incorporeal, i.e. a non-bodily substance) survives and goes on elsewhere. It is the 'soul' or mind which is truly the individual and hence each individual survives death as a disembodied soul. This idea originated with the Greek philosophers and, in particular, Plato. Its most important exponent in recent times was René Descartes who maintained a DUALIST position (dualists maintain that there are, fundamentally, two irreduceable things in the universe – mind and matter – and neither one can be reduced to the other).

This idea still enjoys widespread popular acceptance. Bereaved people often talk of the dead person's 'spirit' or 'soul' going on elsewhere and consider that this spirit, and not the body that lies in the mortuary, is the real individual. There are, however, real difficulties with the dualist position. The main problems include:

(i) The problem of how mind and body interact in a person. Given that mind and body are separate, some interaction between the two is clearly essential. Descartes considered that a small gland at the back of the neck called the 'pineal gland' connected mind and body, but this would not do and the problem of how interaction takes place is still considerable. The mind, after all, is meant to be 'driving' the machine of the human body and yet is separate from the body.

(ii) In a famous book called *The Concept of Mind* (Penguin 1970), Gilbert Ryle rejected the whole idea of a 'ghost in the machine' as he termed the dualist ideas based on Descartes. He said that these ideas rested on a 'category mistake'. Imagine that you are showing a foreigner round a university – you show him the libraries, the college buildings, the playing fields, etc., and having been shown all these the foreigner asks, 'Yes, I have seen all these, but where is the university?' The mistake the foreigner is making is to assume that the university is some thing beyond the accumulation of buildings, etc. which make it up. The parallel is with the human soul. If we look at a human being we can explain everything about him or her in terms which refer to the human person as an individual. Thus we can say that a person thinks, loves, cares, walks, acts, contemplates, etc. If, having explained all these things, someone still demands talk of a 'soul' he or she is, in Ryle's view, making a 'category mistake'. According to Ryle the human person is a unity. Ryle is thus a MONIST (as opposed to a dualist, a monist believes that there are not two things in the universe but only one – in Ryle's case this is matter, although it is also possible to be a monist who believes that only minds exists and that matter is a projection of mind).

(iii) Modern medicine has shown that states of the brain directly affect the way that a person behaves, thinks, relates to others, etc. An operation on the brain can alter a person's personality or destroy his or her memories. The brain, however, is part of the body – it is made up of matter. Given that it is the brain which is the seat of mental activity, emotions, memory and actions, what then becomes of the disembodied soul? Why is it necessary to think in terms of a separate soul at all and, if the brain has died with the body, how can 'I' survive if my brain does not?

(iv) If a 'soul' survives death as a disembodied individual, there are very real problems as to what sort of life this soul could live. How would it communicate with others? How could it have new experiences (as it has no sense organs)? Would it have any location or position and, if so, would it have some sort of 'spiritual body' and, if so, what sort would this be and how would a disembodied soul and a spiritual body interact? There is no space here to deal with these issues in any detail, but the problems are considerable. H. H. Price ('Survival and the idea of Another World' in John Donnelly's *Language, Metaphysics and Death*, Fordham University Press 1978) set out to show what disembodied existence could be like and painted a picture which was not at all attractive – the disembodied soul would be incapable of new experiences and would have to rely on memory. Telepathy would be possible between disembodied souls, but otherwise no new experiences would occur. The soul would be confined to an 'image world' and the individual would literally have made its own heaven or hell by virtue of the memories taken by the soul beyond the grave. The picture Price paints is conceivable, if not very attractive.

(b) The second alternative is to say that a human body is necessary to be a person but, on death, the soul (which is the 'form of the whole body' and not something which is separate and interacts with the body) can survive by itself. On Aquinas's view it is this 'soul' which survives death and passes to purgatory. This 'soul' is only partly the person and it is reunited with a new and glorified body at the time of the second coming or the 'general judgement'. Aquinas says that 'My soul is not I'; until the soul is reunited with the new body at the second coming, it is not fully 'I'. However Aquinas considers that it is the soul which goes to purgatory and the individual is in purgatory. His position is not, therefore, satisfactory. On the one hand the individual survives death as a 'soul' and on the other hand 'my soul is not I'.

Probably the main reason that Aquinas was forced into this unsatisfactory position was because of his need to preserve the idea of two judgements after death – the particular and the general judgements. If there was only one judgement, the whole idea of a disembodied soul could be dispensed with and the philosophic problems much reduced.

(c) The third alternative is to maintain that a person is a person. A person is not made up of soul and body in any form. When a person dies, the person is dead. There is no 'incorporeal substance' which somehow separates from the body. If, therefore, the individual is to survive death, the whole body must be resurrected. The Christian creed affirms the resurrection of the body and could, therefore, be seen to support this approach.

It is worth commenting on just how remarkable it was for the Christian Church to claim that the body was raised from the dead. The creeds were formulated in a world in which Greek philosophic ideas held sway, and the Greeks considered that the real 'I' was the soul. The soul, therefore, was what survived and the body was merely a shell which the soul inhabited. This apparently plausible view the Christian Church rejected, instead maintaining that the whole body was raised from the dead. At the time, this must have seemed much the least likely option, yet today it is generally regarded as the most credible of the possibilities. This does not mean that there are still not many dualists around, but amongst philosophers they tend to be in a distinct minority.

One of the biggest problems which philosophers are concerned about in dealing with the question of survival after death, is the criteria for personal identity. What is it that makes 'me' to be 'me'? This is a much debated question. Various possibilities have been put forward including the idea that identity rests on character, memory, the logical possibility of memory (thus if an old man forgets his childhood memories he could still be the same person as it is logically possible for him to remember) and spatio-temporal continuity. It is almost impossible to give a precise definition of what makes a person, and therefore the search is for the 'necessary but not sufficient conditions' for identity. In other words what are the essential conditions that must be satisfied if the X that survives death is to be the Peter Vardy that died.

All the above possibilities have their share of problems. Character can change even over an individual's life time and is, therefore, not a good test for identity; memory can be mistaken, and if memory is the test of identity the ridiculous situation could arise in which several people remembered exactly the same things and would hence be, on this criterion, all the 'same person'; the logical possibility of memory suffers from the same difficulties and the demand that spatio-temporal continuity is necessary appears to rule out survival after death since an individual's body dies, is buried and decays thus destroying the continuity (unless you maintain a dualist position).

It is important to remember that when Christianity or the other monotheistic religions (monotheism = belief in one God) claim a life after death, the action of a God is generally involved – whether such a God is conceived as personal and everlasting or as timeless substance. A helpful way to think of survival after death may be by using the model of a modern micro-computer. I have a twin-disc drive computer with a printer attached in my college office. When students submit an essay I return this with a sheet of detailed comments. These comments are stored on a computer disc and, by pressing a button on the computer, the comments are printed out. The computer disc contains detailed information instructing the printer how the essay comments are to be spaced out, what type face is to be used and what the punctuation should be. Imagine now that a student loses the essay comments. He or she can then come and ask for a copy. All I have to do is to press a button and exactly the same set of essay comments will be printed out. The layout, spacing, punctuation, etc. will all be identical to the first sheet. It is true that a different sheet of paper will be used, but this is not the important factor. The sheet of essay comments can also be transmitted down a telephone line to another computer or even beamed to the other side of the world via a satellite link-up with, again, the 'same' comments being printed out at the end.

We can now use this example to draw a parallel with God and an individual dying. Assuming God is in some way other than the world and that he can act, then this God would presumably know each and every individual in great detail. He or she would be known through and through: every thought, every characteristic, every memory – in short the whole 'specification' of the person. If an individual then dies, God could presumably recreate the same person using new materials. Christians have never maintained that the same molecules will be used for the resurrected body. St Paul talks of a new and glorified body and new materials are presumably appropriate. (Indeed the molecules making up an individual's body change completely every seven years, so this change of material even happens within an individual's life on earth. It is for this reason that the molecules making up a person are not important in terms of identity; just as the sheet of paper on which the essay comments in the example above are printed is not the crucial factor.)

An individual could, therefore, die here and find him or herself recreated with a new body somewhere else. Given that the individual had the memories of his life here on earth (and these memories would, I suggest, be a necessary condition for talk of personal survival as an individual), then the individual could surely be held to have survived death.

It may, of course, be argued that the 'same' individual has not survived, but rather that an 'identical' individual has been created. If God can recreate the 'same' individual, then, presumably, he could create many identical individuals just as my computer could print out many of the 'same' sheets of essay comments. This is undoubtedly true, but the believer could simply maintain that God, being God, would not do this and would ensure that only one 'new' individual came into existence for each one who died on earth. On this view, there would be continuity between the pre-mortem 'I' and the post-mortem 'I' – the continuity is through the detailed specification of each individual which is held in the mind of God.

The rejection of the dualist position as well as the problems of identity before and after death are among the factors that have led some philosophers to reject the idea of the individual surviving death in any form and hence to see 'eternal life' only as a quality of life here and now. The philosophic problems with this view are, of course, much less than with the idea of personal survival of death but it is open for debate as to whether it is a religiously adequate account.

4 Summary

Eternal life may be seen in three ways:

(a) Eternal life can be seen as a different quality of life that commences now but continues after death in an everlasting heavenly kingdom. This view is likely to be held by those who see God as an everlasting, personal individual,

(b) Eternal life can be seen as a different quality of life that commences now but is fulfilled after death in the timeless beatific vision. This view is likely to be held by those who consider God to be timeless substance or pure act.

(c) Eternal life can be seen as a different quality of life here and now only – drawing on biblical passages such as John 17:3. Believers in all four of the views of God can hold this view, but believers in God as a reality within religious language or in talk of God as affirming a different way of looking at the world are restricted to this view alone. There are no problems of survival after death to deal with.

If either the first or second alternatives are taken, then consideration will also have to be given to what it is that survives death and to what sense can be given to the claim that pre-mortem X is the same individual as post-mortem X. If the third view is taken by itself (i.e. no life after death is accepted), then it must be recognised that the many passages in the New Testament which affirm such an existence will have to be 'explained away'.

7

Evil

1 The problem stated

The existence of evil poses the greatest threat to the credibility of the idea of God seen as an everlasting individual or as timeless substance. In its basic form, the problem can be stated by means of four simple propositions:

(a) God is omnipotent (i.e. God is all-powerful and can thus do everything);
(b) God is completely good;
(c) a completely good, all powerful God would prevent evil;
(d) yet evil exists.

Many religious believers feel that they are committed to holding the first two of these statements to be true. Indeed, if these two statements are denied then it can be questioned whether God is, indeed, 'God'. If God is not omnipotent, then he may become just a very powerful being whom we should, perhaps respect or fear but certainly not worship. Similarly if God is not completely good, then why should a believer worship him? If the second premise above is denied, then there really is little difference between God and the devil. The difference between the two rests on the goodness of the former and the evil ways of the latter. If God is not good, or if he is only partly good, then the dividing line between God and the devil becomes obscured.

The third of the propositions above is more questionable, although it can be held to follow on from the first two. Once, however, the first three propositions are accepted, then evil should not exist – yet most people would say that evil most certainly does exist. If, then, evil exists, the philosopher can argue that one of the three propositions *must* be false. In other words, either:

– God is not all-powerful (and in this case he ceases to be God); or
– God is not completely good (and in this case it is difficult to see why he should be worshipped); or
– a completely good, all-powerful God would choose *not* to eliminate evil (and this seems to be a contradiction).

The problem of evil, therefore, poses a very real challenge to the believer. It is not just a challenge like that presented by prayer where the believer is asked to give a clear account of what happens in prayer and finds this difficult to do (at least based on some of the possible conceptions of God that we have looked at). It is much more serious than that. If the above approach succeeds, it necessarily entails that the believer's claim to worship an all-powerful and completely good God is fundamentally incoherent and must be rejected by any rational individual.

Having posed the basic problem we need to examine the issues in considerably more depth, as it is far from as simple as the above account appears to suggest. To do this, we shall first look at the conceptions of God that are involved and will then examine each of the above propositions in turn before summarising the position at the end of the chapter.

2 The different conceptions of God

One of the principle attractions of rejecting the idea of God as an everlasting individual or as timeless substance and instead affirming that God is an existent reality found within the language of the believing community or that talk of God is a way of affirming a possible way in which life can be lived is that, on the latter two approaches, the problem of evil simply does not arise. Evil is only a problem for the believer if he or she thinks of God as capable, in some sense, of acting in the world. If God is a reality to which the believer can relate his or her life, this can provide depth and content to religious belief, but it does mean that there is no God who is in any sense 'out there', who created the world and who can therefore be held to be responsible for the way things are on earth.

Stewart Sutherland (in *God, Jesus and Belief*) maintains that one of his principal reasons for considering that a revised account of Christian belief is necessary is that the existing idea of God held by believers is untenable. It is untenable largely because no satisfactory solution has been found to the problem of evil. The greater, therefore, the failure to deal with the problem of evil by believers in God seen as an everlasting individual or as timeless substance, the greater is the incentive to opt for one of the alternative accounts of God.

The whole discussion of the problem of evil in this chapter, therefore, rests on one of two assumptions. Either God is an everlasting individual (ch. 3 (1)), or God is timeless substance (ch. 3 (2)) and it makes sense to maintain that such a God can act in the world of time (see ch. 4 for a discussion on this problem). Unless one of these assumptions is held, the problem of evil does not arise. Those who, therefore, consider God to be adequately defined in other terms can read this chapter in the confident knowledge that this is a problem that they do not have to wrestle with since, on the view they have taken of God, the problem does not arise!

3 *God's omnipotence*

The first of the four propositions listed at the beginning of this chapter was: God is omnipotent (i.e. God is all-powerful and can thus do everything). The first question that needs then to be asked is: What is meant by 'everything'? The problem is illustrated by many of the well-known schoolroom dilemmas that are meant to confront God, for instance:

– Can God make a square circle?
– Can God make a stone that is too heavy for him to lift?
– Can God climb a tree?
– Can God commit suicide?

There are two possible views of what it means to say that God can do 'everything' depending on whether he can or cannot do the 'logically impossible'. Something is logically impossible if it contradicts the rules of logic. For instance, in logic, something cannot be all black and all white at the same time or, to put it another way, P (where P represents any positive statement) can never equal not-P. Either:

(a) God can do everything, absolutely. This view was put forward by Descartes and it maintains that God can do the logically impossible. God can, in other words, make P = not-P. On this view God can, indeed, make a square circle. Or:

(b) God can only do the logically possible. This was Aquinas' view. He considered that to say that God can do the logically impossible is to talk nonsense. Effectively there can be no such thing as a square circle and, therefore, it is no limitation on God's omnipotence to say that he cannot create it. It is rather like saying that God cannot make a mouse who is six feet tall, can gallop like a horse and do advanced physics at the same time. If there were such a creature, it would not be a mouse! Similarly a circle has no angles – a square has four angles and it is simply nonsense to say that the two ideas can be combined.

I am going to assume, for the moment without argument, that the second of these two approaches is the right one. I will justify this assumption later, but if any reader *does* maintain that God can do the logically impossible, I will be arguing that this view provides total and complete proof that God either does not exist or is fundamentally evil! The first proposition needs, therefore, to be modified to:

God is omnipotent (i.e. God can do anything that is logically possible).

4 God's goodness

The second of the two propositions at the beginning of this chapter was that: God is completely good.

The problem here is to know what is meant by 'good'. At

first sight this may seem obvious, but in fact it is far from clear. Consider the following:

- Luke is a good boy.
- Rover is a good dog.
- This is good cheese.
- She is good at fiddling her income tax returns.
- Divorce is good if a marriage has irrevocably broken down.
- An inoculation is good for you.

'Good' is a word that cannot be analysed any further and it has different meanings depending on the sentence and the context. What we regard as 'good' may change over time. We do not have space here to enter into the complex ethical issues that centre on the idea of 'goodness', but it is important to recognise that ideas of what is good vary considerably and there will often be widespread disagreement about what is and what is not good.

Having said this, there may be general agreement about what is good and what is bad and this agreement may rest on our common humanity. Thus, beating up babies for pleasure after lunch on Sunday afternoons would generally be regarded as bad whilst helping someone who is in danger might be regarded as good. However even these apparently obvious cases are not necessarily as clear-cut as they may seem. In some societies, helping others is not a priority nor, indeed, is there any moral impulse to act in this way. Each person may be regarded as being in a certain position in life because of his or her actions, either in this life or in a previous one, and he or she must simply take the consequences. It is all too easy to generalise from a Western perspective and to assume that this perspective applies everywhere in the world.

Kant provided one of the clearest and most general principles on which morality rested. Kant sought not to lay down moral rules but to determine the principles on which all morality is based. In *Groundwork of the Metaphysics of Morals*, he produced various formulations of his 'categorical imperative'. This, in his view, represented the general principle underlying morality. This principle was 'categorical' as it was not undertaken for some other reason – it was an unconditional demand.

The principles on which most people act are generally 'hypothetical'; to take an example, if I say, 'If you want to stay healthy, you should reduce your sugar and salt intake', the injunction to reduce your sugar and salt intake is based on an 'if' – that you want to stay healthy. This would, therefore, be an example of a hypothetical command; it is a command based on a reason. By contrast, moral demands are not hypothetical but categorical. Thus if someone says 'Why should I not beat up babies on Sunday afternoons', the answer is *not* to give a reason (if a reason is given then the reason may be rejected and hence the command with it); rather it is simply the case that *this is wrong*. It is wrong for no other reason than that this is a wrong action. Morality is thus a categorical imperative – a command to action based on no reason outside itself. Morality rests on reason. A wholly rational individual will be moral not for some ulterior motive but because reason will lead him or her to act in accordance with morality's demands.

Kant put forward several versions of the categorical imperative, but these effectively included:

– Treat people always as ends, never as means to some end. (In other words people should always be treated as of vital importance and value in their own right; they should never be used as a means to some other end.)
– Act in such a way that you can will that the maxim of your action should be a universal law. (To put this more clearly, this might be expressed by saying, 'Always act in such a way that you can will that everyone else placed in the same situation should also act similarly.')

This is not the place to debate the merits of the categorical imperative, but the important point to note is that this and every other general principle of morality governs relationships between human beings. Our ideas of what is good are based on morality and, therefore, on relationships between human beings here on earth.

When we say 'God is good', if this is to mean the same as 'Luke is a good boy', then God's goodness becomes a matter of wanting whatever is best for mankind here on earth, since we derive our ideas of goodness from whatever is for the good of man. Christianity, however, has always affirmed that what the world regards as best and what God regards as best are two entirely different things. The world generally seeks pleasure and an elimination of pain; it seeks to avoid suffering and hardships. Christianity, however, points to a straight and narrow road which few will wish to travel, and it affirms that God's ways are not the ways of man.

Imagine a tadpole pool. Within the pool, morality represents the rules that govern relationships between the tadpoles. A good tadpole is one who fosters the good of the other tadpoles in the pool. If, however, the destiny of tadpoles is not to live and die in the pool but rather to grow to become frogs, then what appears good for the tadpoles within the pool may not, in fact, be so. The parallel, of course, is with man – if this life is all there is, then what is good for man will be determined solely within this world. If, however, man's eventual destiny is to be found in fellowship with God after death, then God may look at things in an entirely different way to us. It follows, therefore, that the believer who asserts that 'God is good' may not be claiming that God wants the same things for us as we want for ourselves. God has a different order of priorities, a different way of looking at the world.

This view can be seen to be affirmed by those who hold that God is timeless and that language about God is metaphorical and not univocal. When, on this view, the believer says that 'God is good', he or she may be saying something that is true but not literally true in the way we normally use language. The believer may be maintaining that God is indeed good but his goodness is other than ours, that it operates from a different perspective and from a wider viewpoint. It follows, therefore, that things that may appear to us to be bad (such as illness or pain) may, from God's point of view, not necessarily be so. These can provide opportunities for growth and development that an individual may not realise at the time.

The second of the four propositions set out at the beginning of this chapter needs, therefore, to be modified on the following lines:

God is completely good, but as his viewpoint is different

from ours, what God knows to be good may, at the time, seem to us to be bad.

5 *A completely good God would eliminate evil*

The central issue raised by this premise is the question of human freedom. Assuming that the believer believes in a God apart from the universe who can act in the world (i.e. either an everlasting individual or timeless substance), then this God could clearly have created robots in human form who would always do what was right. However, *if* such a God wished to create men who would be genuinely free to choose whether or not to love him, whether to enter into a relationship with him which can begin in this world but continue after death, then the problem becomes more complex.

If man is to be genuinely free, then God (*if* he can only do the logically possible) has no choice but to allow man to exercise this freedom. This is the core of the 'free-will defence' against the problem of evil. The free-will defence maintains that:

(a) The highest good is that man should enter into a personal, loving relationship with God.
(b) This relationship is only possible if man is genuinely free to choose whether to love God or to ignore him, and this choice is not wholly determined by a person's background or genetic make-up.
(c) Once man is given this freedom by God, then God cannot stop man exercising it without destroying the possibility of (a) above,
(d) Evil therefore occurs as a result of the free choices made by man.

This defence succeeds in that it shows why an omnipotent, all-good God should allow evil to take place. God may regret this evil and he may wish it to stop, but he is unable to do so *except* by depriving human beings of their freedom and thus preventing them from entering into a free and loving relationship with him. This is where the view taken of God's omnipotence becomes so important. If one holds, with

Descartes, that God can do the logically impossible, then there is no reason at all why he should not have made men genuinely free to choose how to act *and* ensured that men only do what is right.

This would, of course, be the best of all situations, but it is logically impossible. One *cannot* allow someone to be completely free *and* ensure that they act in a certain way. This amounts to a contradiction in terms. The only way that God could do this would be if God could do the logically impossible. *If* one maintains that God can do the logically impossible, then his failure to bring about the above two states of affairs proves that he cannot be all-good. However, if it is nonsense (as Aquinas maintained) to talk of God doing the logically impossible, then the free-will defence is valid and succeeds – at least up to a point.

The point which the free-will defence fails to cover is the existence of natural evil. There are two broad categories of evil:

- MORAL EVIL, i.e. evil that man can be held to be responsible for. The free-will defence deals with this provided that God can only do the logically possible.
- NATURAL EVIL, e.g. earthquakes, volcanoes, tidal-waves, illness and similar events brought about by natural forces that are beyond man's control.

Richard Swinburne has argued (in *The Existence of God*, Oxford 1979) that the world we have is exactly the sort of world that God would have cause to create. It is a world where natural laws operate regularly, where man can discover these laws and learn to cope with them, where these laws create disasters which can have terrible consequences but which provide opportunities for bravery, self-sacrifice, etc. Swinburne rejects the view of those who maintain that the limits of suffering caused by natural disasters are too wide. He says that people who hold this view are arguing for a 'toy world' where nothing matters very much, where there are few opportunities for self-sacrifice, bravery, etc. God has, Swinburne maintains, set limits to human suffering – human life has a relatively short span so the length of suffering is limited and a human being passes out when pain reaches a certain intensity.

Swinburne's view depends on a judgement of how much evil is tolerable, and this is more a question of opinion than philosophic analysis. I have to say, however, that his view seems to me to verge on the obscene. To be able to hold that God has set acceptable limits to human suffering as one watches an individual whom one loves die in agony from cancer or one sees the pictures from Auschwitz, seems particularly far-fetched. Having said this, Swinburne does at least try to provide an answer.

Another way of approaching the problem of natural evil is derived from Aquinas and is sometimes taken by those who affirm that God is timeless substance. Such a God can, as we saw in chapter 3, never change in any way. The believer does not know what God is, but he or she does know that God is fully whatever it is to be God. God is fully actual (he is 'pure act'), he has no potential to be other than he is. If this timeless God is to show his greatness and power in the universe that he has made, then it follows that he will create a hierarchy of goods – the larger the range of creatures and things the better. If God was restricted to only creating creatures and things that were perfect then this would, indeed, impose limits on his power. Unless you have death you cannot have birth, unless you have winter, you cannot have spring. God, therefore, shows his greatness and his goodness by creating a vastly diverse universe with a tremendous range of creatures and things which exhibit goodness in varying degrees. 'Evil', on this view, is one of two things:

(a) A falling short (or 'privation') of what it is to be fully whatever God intended. Thus, to the extent that man is less than fully what man has the ability to become, man will be evil. Man is intended for relationship to and fellowship with God, so to the extent that he rejects this he falls short of the true possibilities inherent in his nature and is therefore evil. Or:

(b) Evil is the term given by man to natural events which appear inconvenient to him but which are not evil in themselves. When seen from the correct perspective the whole of nature can be seen as showing forth a vast array of different forms of goodness. A world with volcanoes, earthquakes, tidal waves, death and disease does, on this view, provide greater opportunities for the manifestation of God's goodness than would a perfect and static universe.

Again, according to this view, we have the idea of God's goodness being 'other than' goodness as it is normally understood.

This view admits that God created the universe as it is with all the potential for natural disasters that man finds within it, but sees this as part of God's purpose to manifest his goodness more clearly. Those who reject this view could claim that an omnipotent God could, surely, have created a universe which still shows his power but without the terrible suffering that disease and other natural disasters bring to mankind.

In sum, therefore, believers would want to modify the third of the propositions with which we started this chapter as follows:

A completely good, all powerful God would prevent evil as far as it is in his power to do so. However, given that he can only do the logically possible, he has to allow people freedom to act as they wish and hence to bring about moral evil.

Natural evil, however, is more difficult to explain except on the basis that God had to allow this amount of evil in order to foster the higher human virtues or to manifest his power to best effect. The believer may well find natural evil inexplicable but will nevertheless continue to trust and believe in God, while the non-believer may see the existence of this evil as good grounds for rejecting belief in God conceived as an everlasting individual or as timeless substance. Much is, therefore, going to depend on the individual's presuppositions.

6 Is it all worth it?

In Dostoyevsky's *The Brothers Karamazov*, the story is told of two brothers, Ivan and Alyosha. Aloysha is a novice monk, a quiet, good and dedicated man. The two brothers meet after an absence of some years and Ivan explains to Alyosha why he rejects God. He says that he accepts that God exists, but he rejects the world that God has made. He tells several stories of the suffering of innocent children which appal Alyosha. In one, a young child is torn to pieces (while his parents are forced to watch) by a pack of hounds owned by a local lord because the child had hurt the leg of one of the lord's dogs. In another a group of soldiers made babies smile before blowing their eyes out with their guns.

Ivan says that he rejects the God who could create a world where such suffering could take place. The depth and subtlety of his attack is based on the view that, even though man may be free, it was God who created the world. God is omniscient (i.e. he knows everything) so he must have known how men would misuse their freedom. It is not open to God to claim ignorance, since God knows everything in the future and the past. While, therefore, the free-will defence may appear to work, Ivan effectively argues that it does not do so. It is as if I gave a loaded gun to my three-year-old daughter and sent her out to play with her friends. If she then kills one of them, I cannot blame her. It was I who gave her the gun and I must take responsibility. In the same way God must take the responsibility for man's free decisions.

Ivan argues that the whole of God's creation needs to be rejected. Genesis says that God saw what he had made and it was good. Ivan maintains that it was very bad indeed. What is more, Ivan rejects any attempt by the believer to say that some future beatific vision or some heavenly kingdom to come will make all the suffering worth while. Nothing, in his view, is worth the suffering of one innocent child.

This is a very powerful attack, and it can be made even more so if we consider a contemporary example. Imagine you have a young and innocent teenage daughter. A thoroughly unpleasant and unprincipled man approaches her and asks her to go to bed with him. She knows this is totally wrong as well as being repulsive to her. The man offers to pay £100,000 to the favourite charity of her choice if she will agree. He might say: 'I know you consider this to be wrong, but what you must remember is the good that will come from it. With £100,000, the lives of over a thousand starving people in Africa will be saved or you can choose any other good cause you wish. The evil you have to undergo is a small price compared with the ultimate good that will result.'

The question is, what would you advise your daughter? You have two choices. You can say: (a) What is proposed is evil and wicked. No matter what the benefit to others, you must not do this terrible thing; or (b) What is proposed is evil, however the ultimate good that will result is worth the price.

Many people would opt for (a), yet if they take this position they are likely to be forced to go along with Ivan's rejection of God. If God permits terrible evil and suffering to innocent children to take place in order that a higher good may result in the future (i.e. fellowship with him for those who achieve salvation), then is he not to be rejected and condemned on moral grounds in a similar way by the individual who rejects the proposed action by his or her daughter?

If, on the other hand, an individual says that his or her daughter should take the £100,000 and the consequences that go with it, then Ivan's challenge fails. The issue is really whether it is permissible to allow evil in order that good may come from it. This is what Ivan accuses God of doing and it is this that Ivan rejects.

The problem, therefore, is whether it is 'worth it' or morally permissible for God to have created a world in which he knew that men would inflict hideous sufferings on each other, even if this is the only logically possible way to achieve salvation or fellowship with him for those who desire this. This really rests on a value judgement, and much will depend on which option an individual would choose for his or her daughter!

There are two possible ways out of the dilemma posed by Ivan. First it could be argued that the girl should reject the proposal on the grounds that she does not know the effects of the proposed action on her, on her seducer or on others. God, on the other hand, knows the consequences of allowing evil and is therefore justified in allowing it as he knows that the final outcome is worth the price. Alternatively it might be argued that God did not know what men would do with their freedom. If this is the case, then God cannot be condemned for creating the best of all possible worlds if men choose to act in an appalling way since he did not know what men would do. There are certainly passages in the Bible that would seem to support this view. Thus Genesis says: 'The Lord saw that the wickedness of man was great in the earth, and that every imagination of the thoughts of his heart was only evil continually. And the Lord was sorry that he had made man on the earth, and it grieved him to his heart' (Gen. 6:5–6).

This view is only tenable if God is considered to be an everlasting individual. If God is timeless substance he knows everything equally in the past, present and future. He would know exactly what every single individual would do. If, therefore, God is timeless substance, he is totally omniscient in that he knows everything absolutely and the dilemma posed by Ivan is very real. If, on the other hand, God is in time, then it may be held that it is impossible for him to know future events that have not yet occurred. On this basis the evil that man does to man could genuinely surprise God, as the passage from Genesis suggests.

The problem with this attractive view is that God's knowledge of the future is considerably restricted. God could, however, be like a grand master at chess (as suggested by Peter Geach (*Providence and Evil*, Cambridge 1977)). A grand master may not know what move his opponent will make next but, whatever the move, he plays the game so well that he will ultimately emerge victorious. Similarly God, if he is an everlasting individual, may not know specifically what any individual will do next, but he will nevertheless be able to ensure that his purposes will not be frustrated.

7 Bringing the threads together

The problem of evil only arises if God is either an everlasting individual or timeless substance capable of acting in the world and responsible for its creation. The third and fourth views of God, as set out in chapter 3, have the real advantage that evil is no longer a problem since there is no God 'out there' who created the world.

We have seen in this chapter that the initial propositions which set out the problem of evil need to be modified as follows:

(a) God is omnipotent, i.e. God can do anything that is logically possible. (See section 3 above.)
(b) God is completely good but, as his viewpoint is different from ours, what God knows to be good may, at the time, seem to us to be had. (See section 4 above.)
(c) A completely good, all powerful God would prevent evil as far as it is in his power to do so. However, given that he can only do the logically possible, he has to allow people freedom to act as they wish and hence to bring about moral evil. (See section 5 above.)

The free-will defence was seen to have considerable force in respect of moral evil, but no satisfactory answer was found to explain natural evil except, possibly, that this form of evil is necessary in order that the higher virtues can be possible for man or that God creates things which appear evil to us as a way of manifesting his power and goodness in the universe. Both these views have difficulties.

The challenge posed by Ivan (in Dostoyevsky's *The Brothers Karamazov*) that no eventual state of fulfilment or salvation could justify the suffering of innocent children posed a real dilemma, and here the reader must decide whether it can be justifiable to allow evil in order that good may come. One way out of this problem is to maintain that God is an everlasting individual who does not know exactly what will happen in the future, although he is still able to ensure that his eventual purposes are not frustrated, whatever man may do. There is biblical backing for this view, but it does mean a real limitation on God's omniscience.

8 The biblical approach

Lastly it would be wrong to leave the problem of evil without looking at the biblical approach to the problem. There are two Old Testament books that are particularly concerned with this issue – Job and Habbakuk. Habbakuk was a prophet at the time of the Babylonian captivity. The Israelites had been taken captive, their cities destroyed, their kingdom vanquished and their people led off to slavery. Habbakuk knows that God is real, that he is all powerful and is a God of love. How, then is the success of the Babylonians to be explained? His book is a meditation on this but, in the end, no answer is given to the prophet except that 'the righteous shall live by his faith'. This famous phrase was influential in the New Testament and also provided a touchstone for the reformers at the time of the Reformation. The righteous man must live quietly in obedience to and trust in God, knowing that there are mysteries (including evil) that he cannot understand.

The book of Job is better known than Habbakuk. Job is held up by God as an example of righteousness. Even when Satan takes away all his possessions and inflicts terrible sufferings on Job, even when his friends try to show him the futility of continued loyalty to God, Job refuses to turn aside from the righteous path. In a magnificent speech in the final chapters of the book, God replies to the charges made against him. However, God refuses any explanation. His reply rather takes the form of getting Job to see just how small and insignificant he is and how totally he is unable to understand the ways of God. As an example, God says to Job:

'Where were you when I laid the foundations of the earth?
    Tell me if you have understanding.
Who determined its measurements – surely you know!
    Or who stretched the line upon it? . . .
Can you bind the chains of the Pleiades
    or loose the cords of Orion? . . .
Do you know when the mountain goats bring forth?
    Do you observe the calving of the hinds? . . .
Is it by your wisdom that the hawk soars,
    and spreads his wings towards the south?
Is it at your command that the eagle mounts up
    and makes his nest on high? . . .'
And the Lord said to Job: 'Shall a faultfinder contend
    with the Almighty?
He who argues with God let him answer it.'
                    (from Job, chs. 38—40)

In other words the Bible recognises the problem of evil and says that the believer is entirely right to be aware of it. However, no answer will be given. Some things man cannot understand – and the existence of evil is one of them.

8

Religious Experience

1 What is religious experience?

In a radio debate with Bertrand Russell, Father Copleston sj defined religious experience as follows:

> By religious experience I don't mean simply feeling good.
> I mean a loving but unclear awareness of some object
> which irresistibly seems to the experiencer as something
> transcending the self, something which cannot be pictured
> or conceptualised, but of the reality of which doubt is
> impossible – at least during the experience. I should claim
> that this cannot be explained adequately and without
> residue simply subjectively.

It is important to note Copleston's stress on 'without residue'.
He could accept that some 'religious experiences' may be due
to psychological or subjective factors or even to the influence
of certain drugs. However his point is that although many
and various explanations may be given for these religious
experiences, these explanations cannot explain them
completely. There is 'more to' the experiences than these
explanations allow.

To talk of 'religious experiences' in general terms can be
unhelpful, as there is such a wide spread of experiences that
are described as 'religious', and greater clarity is needed.
Richard Swinburne in his book *The Existence of God* (pp. 249 –
53) has a useful analysis of the different categories of religious
experience. He describes five types – the first two are public
experiences, in that they would be experienced by anyone
who was in the right place at the right time, and the last
three are private, interior experiences. All five can fittingly

be described as 'religious', but by breaking down the experiences in this way it can help the individual to become clearer about just what type of experience he or she may be discussing. Swinburne's categories are as follows:

Public experiences:

(a) Where an individual 'sees' God or God's action in a public object or scene. For instance a believer might 'see' the hand of God when looking at the night sky or a pastoral scene. The non-believer could clearly see the same scene and not 'see' God or God's action in any way. Everything, therefore, depends on the interpretation brought to the experience and it is in this interpretation that believer and non-believer will differ (cf. Wisdom's example of the 'invisible gardener' referred to in ch. 4).

(b) Experiences of very unusual public objects which may involve breaches of an apparent natural law, such as walking on water, resurrection appearances, figures appearing in locked rooms, etc. In the case of these experiences, there is less dependence of interpretation, although the sceptic can still challenge the experience. Thus if the believer sees a holy man walking on water, he or she may be prepared to see this as a religious experience of a manifestation of God's power. The sceptic, however, whilst admitting the experience may look for a natural explanation – for instance to see whether the man is walking on something beneath the waves or even is being supported by unseen force fields of some sort!

Private experiences (these, by their very nature, are less prone to verification than public experiences seen by other people):

(c) Experiences which an individual can describe using normal terms. Thus Jacob's description of his dream and of a ladder going up and down to heaven is a private experience which is nevertheless described in terms which everyone can recognise and accept. Some people have vivid dreams which they can remember and which can be described in these terms.

   In the case of dreams, it is difficult to separate 'I

94

dreamed that I saw the Virgin Mary' from 'The Virgin Mary appeared to me while I was asleep'. However experiences under this heading need not be confined to dreams and can include any private religious experience which can be described within normal language.

(d) Experiences which cannot be described in normal language but which nevertheless do constitute a specific experience. Examples might be a feeling of peace or contentment, an apprehension of the fundamental unity and 'oneness' of all things or a sense of awe. The individual who has such an experience can use ordinary language but cannot specifically describe the experience – he will have to use analogies and 'pictures' to help his or her hearer to understand what the experience was like. Many mystical experiences might come under this heading – for instance, where the mystic tries to talk of a sense of nothingness in which God is nevertheless wholly present.

(e) The fifth category hardly deserves the title 'experience' at all, since there is no specific experience to which it relates. Rather, the individual feels that God is acting in some way in his or her life or is in some way affecting the individual. Thus the individual may look back over his or her life and may claim that God has acted to bring certain things about or to be particularly near the individual at crucial times. However, no specific experience could be pointed to in support of this claim. It rather rests on an 'awareness' which has no specific form and cannot, therefore, be adequately described. In the end, the believer who claims such a religious experience may be totally convinced about it, but may find it almost impossible to communicate to others what it was that led him or her to describe the experience as coming from God.

It is worth being clear which heading any claimed experience falls under, as the problems will be different with each heading. In the case of public experiences there will first be a need to establish the accuracy of the reported experience and secondly to discuss the interpretation of these facts. The sceptic can simply dismiss the private experiences as never

having occurred or as being purely the product of psychological or other factors. Adolescent girls, for instance, sometimes report experiences which might be described as
'religious' and these might be explained in terms of hormone
changes. We do know that many reported mystical states can
be duplicated with the use of drugs, and the sceptic can
therefore accept that mystical experiences occur but deny that
they should be termed 'religious' as they can be explained by
psychological factors.

One possible problem with Swinburne's analysis is that it
can appear to make religious experiences very similar to any
other experiences. The idea of what Otto termed 'an apprehension of the wholly other' or any feeling of awe or wonder
seems to be largely missing. What, in other words, marks a
particular experience as being 'religious' in character? Much
is going to depend on the interpretation that the individual
brings to the experience, and this raises a major issue –
whether religious experience serves as a foundation for faith
or whether these experiences only occur to those who already
believe on other grounds.

2 Foundation or part of the building?

Do religious experiences act as a foundation for faith,
providing a basis for belief and commitment or do they rather
only occur when believers are committed to belief on other
grounds (whatever these other grounds may be)?

St Ambrose said: 'It has not pleased God to save his people
with arguments.' Many people who consider that the arguments for the existence of God are not convincing to someone
who does not already believe, maintain that religious experience provides the foundation for faith. This is a very
important issue, as *if* the arguments for the existence of God
are not convincing to a rational, uncommitted individual,
why should anyone believe other than because they have been
brought up within a particular faith?

It must be recognised that many people do share the beliefs
of their parents, but of course there are conversions and
people do lapse from the faith that they have been brought
up in. However, in percentage terms the majority of people

who worship in different churches do so because their parents did so or because they went to a school where they learnt the teachings of this church. It is only a small minority who actually make a rational decision between different churches or between different religions. If, therefore, religious experience does serve as a foundation for faith, this can provide a justification for the believer's claim to believe. We need to consider whether religious experience does operate in this way.

The paradigm case of a conversion brought about by a religious experience is often taken as that of St Paul. However, while this may seem to provide a clear-out example, the position is much less straightforward when it is analysed. The Acts of the Apostles gives three different accounts of Paul's conversion experience and they are all different. It is almost as if the writer of Acts did not think it important to get the accounts to agree. On the face of it, the experience on the Damascus road fits into the second of the categories set out in the previous section; in other words, it was public and unusual (light and sound). In the first account (ch. 9) those who were with Paul heard the voice from heaven, in chapter 22 Paul says that those with him did not hear the voice but only saw a light, and in chapter 26 the position is not clear. The distinctive part of the experience was, therefore, either private to Paul (ch. 22) or public (ch. 9).

There are various possibilities as to what happened to Paul. All versions agree that there was a great light of some sort, then the three accounts differ:

(a) There was a voice from heaven which everyone heard. If this was, indeed, the case and if we had supporting evidence from those who were with Paul, this might well provide evidence in favour of the experience having taken place as described. The problem, of course, is that we have no such evidence.

(b) There was a voice which only Paul heard. In this case we are entirely dependent on Paul's account.

(c) Paul thought that he heard a voice. He may not have done so and, for instance, the 'voice' may have been the realisation that came to him on the road that he had been wrong to persecute the Christians. He may have been reflecting on the death of Stephen and have come to the conclusion that he was acting against God rather than serving him. This sudden realisation could have had a tremendous effect on Paul and, with his usual energy, he could have decided to totally transform his life and proclaim Christianity instead of persecuting its followers.

It does not seem to matter which of these views is taken. Even if (c) is the chosen option, the believer could say that God brought Paul to realise the error of his ways. It is thus not the content but the effect of the conversion experience on Paul that is decisive. Something happened to him, and whatever it was caused a total transformation of his life. The experience can rightly be described as 'religious' because Paul related the experience to God and it brought about a transformation of his life.

Paul's experience is usually described in terms of 'conversion', but prior to the experience Paul believed in God and God's action in history. He accepted the Old Testament, he knew about Jesus and the teachings of the Christians and was well aware of the relationship between the fledgling Christian Church and the Jewish community. For Paul, therefore, his 'conversion' to Christianity was a reordering of concepts that he already had; it was a matter of seeing the figure of Jesus in a new light, in coming to accept him as coming from God rather than being opposed to God. The step was in one way enormous as it meant abandoning the traditional Jewish approach, but in another way the step was not very large – Christianity just came to be seen as the natural fruition and completion of everything the Old Testament had proclaimed.

Paul's conversion experience may, therefore, have been the occasion for his conversion but it need not be regarded as the foundation for his belief in God. This foundation lay in his Jewish heritage and background, in the teaching he received from his parents and teachers. Today the same situation may apply. Religious experiences (of whatever type) are rarely coercive – they do not compel belief nor do they provide factual information which can act as a groundwork for belief. If this is accepted, religious experience may have three possible roles:

(a) To provide the occasion for a person who has knowledge of a set of religious beliefs to appropriate these beliefs for him or herself and to start living by them. For instance, an experience of the night sky in open countryside might act as the occasion for an individual to reassess his or her life and, where the individual had previously seen no meaning or value in the religious life, he or she might come to see the futility of all that had previously been regarded as important and the necessity to live life henceforward in a different way.

(b) To reinforce existing belief. Thus a believer may have either a single religious experience or a growing sense of awareness of the activity of God in his or her life. Such experiences would serve to reinforce existing beliefs and to engender greater commitment and dedication. The believer might well claim that the beliefs held on other grounds had been justified by the experience he or she had had.

(c) To provide a turning point in a life already dedicated to God. An experience (which, again, can be of various types) may lead to a new direction, a new vocation or a new understanding of what the believer's commitment must mean to him or her.

In all these areas, it is not so much the content of the experience that will be important as the interpretation given to it. The verification of the experience as being truly religious will come not from an analysis of the experience but by looking at the effect it had on the individual's life. St Paul's conversion is a prime case in point – Paul invites those who are judging him to see his whole life in terms of his conversion experience. The whole of his life subsequent to the experience itself provides a validation of the experience, or at least of the effect on Paul of the experience. The outside observer may not be able to determine precisely what happened to Paul, but this is not the important issue. The key factor is that 'something' happened, and whatever this 'something' was, Paul related this to God and the direction of his life was totally transformed as a result.

3 Validating religious experiences

A religious experience may be so overwhelming to the person who has it that doubt is impossible. No amount of psychological analysis, no philosophic questioning will undermine the reality of the experience for the individual concerned. However when the individual tries to communicate this experience, problems are likely to arise and consideration then has to be given as to how 'true' and 'false' religious experiences are to be separated. Various criteria can be suggested which might validate a claim to a religious experience. These include:

(a) Coherence with an existing belief system (e.g. the teachings of the Church or biblical teachings). Paul's experience may not show up well in these terms, as his experience led him away from the Jewish tradition. However, he would certainly have regarded his commitment to Christ as being in accordance with this tradition and his fellow Christians would have agreed with this. Similarly today someone may genuinely feel called by God to renew the Church and this may mean standing against the Church in a prophetic role. The Old Testament prophets were often thorns in the sides of the established authorities and conformity with the *status quo* is not a decisive test for divine inspiration!

(b) Moral criteria. This need not be an inflexible rule. Abraham was called by God to act against morality when he was asked to sacrifice Isaac, and an individual may feel called to respond to a command from God against what may be perceived as his or her moral duty to aged parent or relative. However, morality is clearly one of the factors that needs to be taken into account. Anyone claiming that God has told them to kill should view such a supposed command with very great suspicion and should first think in terms of psychological states or delusion.

(c) The conviction with which the person who claims the experience believes in it and lives his or her life by it. Someone who claims to have been told to do something

by God and then does nothing about it, undermines his
or her own claim by inaction.

(d) Whether the experience can be seen as part of a life
dedicated to the love and service of God. Abraham's call
to sacrifice Isaac could be seen in these terms while a
similar call to someone who had no past history of dedication or religious commitment would need to be viewed
with very great suspicion. Here again, therefore, the claim
to a religious experience by a non-believer, while not
being ruled out, is rendered less plausible.

It is, thus, not so much the *content* of the religious experience
that is decisive but the *effect* that this experience has on the
life of the individual. There are parallels between religious
experiences and UFO sightings. The latter are not available
to everyone (possibly because the spacemen choose not to
reveal themselves); some of the experiences may be indescrib-
able and there may be no agreement on the experiences (some
may see Daleks, others little green men, yet others a saucer
crewed by intelligent spiders). Why should anyone be more
willing to accept a claim to have seen Jesus, the Virgin Mary
or Mohammed rather than little green men? Clearly someone
who believes in the thing being seen will find the reported
sightings more compelling that those who do not believe.
Therefore: if I do not believe that there have been visitors
from another planet, I am likely to be deeply sceptical about
claims to have seen little green men; if I am a Protestant, I
am likely to be sceptical about anyone claiming to have seen
the Virgin Mary who announced herself as 'The Immaculate
Conception'; if I am an atheist, I am likely to be sceptical
about *any* religious experience at all.

The plausibility of reported experiences is thus going to
depend to a large extent on the individual's prior view.
However, scepticism is one thing, and total rejection is
another, and whether an individual will take such reported
experiences seriously may be partly determined by what he
or she knows about the individual concerned and the effect
that the experience may have had on the individual. The
more sane, rational and well known to me an individual is,
the more I am likely to accept what he says. It is, therefore,
possible for one person's reported experience and the convic-

tion with which it is communicated to cause someone else to stop and think. We are not dealing here with absolutes but with a sliding scale.

Jesus said of his followers: 'You will know them by their fruits' (Matt. 7:20). In other words, if someone claims to be a believer in God, his or her life should be transformed and the individual should become a new creature, acting in a different way, caring and being concerned with everyone he or she meets. If this happens, then indeed it may be true (in the words of the hymn) for the believers to say: 'They can tell we are Christians by our love.'

All too often, however, this is not the case. The believer is no different from anyone else; apart from an hour on Sunday, many believers' lives simply reflect the norms of the society in which they live. If this is indeed the position, then any claim by the believer to have 'experienced God' or to be 'aware of God's presence or activity' is largely undermined immediately it is made. If such an experience was real, then it could be expected to have positive fruits – the *effects* would be there to see, not just in words but in actions.

4 Religious experiences and alternative conceptions of God

It might be expected that the four different conceptions of God set out in chapter 2 would have a decisive impact on the type of religious experience that a believer can accept. Certainly there is some effect, but it is not as decisive as may be at first imagined.

Someone who sees God's reality as existing within the language of the believing community can certainly maintain that religious experiences occur. Within the community, God necessarily exists. Whenever two or three are gathered together in God's name, he is there, as a reality which the believers are aware of. If, for instance, a Roman Catholic affirmed this position, he might maintain that God was closest to him or her and was most really present during the Mass, when the bread and wine becomes for the individual the body and the blood of Christ. At this most sacred moment, the believers have united their wills in dedication and obedience to God and it is at this moment that God is most truly real to them.

This (it may be maintained) can give a far more plausible account of the 'real presence' than to maintain that by some miraculous activity of an outside agent the bread and wine has been transformed into flesh and blood while retaining all the outward characteristics of bread and wine. Again, an individual who believes in God as defined under this heading may experience the reality of God at many points in his or her life. As the individual tries to live according to God's will and to actualise Christ's example in his or her life, so the meaning and value of this life may become ever more apparent. The night sky or other natural wonders may also point to the meaninglessness of much human endeavour and emphasise the individual's finitude and the necessity to live a life dedicated to the reality of God.

The believer in God as this form of reality can, indeed, accept four of the five categories of religious experience set out in section 1 above. Only the second type of experience (of very unusual public events such as resurrection appearances, walking on water and the like) would have to be dismissed. There is, after all, no 'Being, Spirit or Individual' in any sense 'out there' under this heading who could intervene in the world and act in this way.

If the fourth view of God is taken (as an alternative view of life seen *sub specie aeternitatis*), then all the above forms of experience could be endorsed. The particular experiences that would be most likely to be described as religious under this heading would be those where the possibility of a transformation of life was seen or where the meaning or course of life was understood clearly. Thus when Jesus prayed in Gethesemane and came to realise through his prayer that he must face crucifixion on the following morning, this could well be described as a religious experience. Life is seen in context, and the individual can see how he or she must act in order to overcome the constraints that time places on his or her life. Such an insight can indeed be uplifting and religious.

To those who regard God as personal and everlasting, the above experiences are all available. In addition, however, such individuals may claim an experience of God in a similar, but less direct, way to having an experience of another individual. This experience may either be mediated or unmediated. The Old Testament maintained that no man can see

God and live; generally any such experience is going to be mediated (for instance, in the case of Moses, it was through the burning bush). In most cases, however, such religious experiences will be a feeling of awareness of God as an individual who is closer to the individual than anything or anyone else. God, in this case, is a personal reality of whom the believer is very much aware, although the number of cases where this awareness will be different from the religious experiences endorsed by those who believe in God as defined above may be fairly restricted.

If God is considered to be timeless substance, then it is questionable to what extent he can be regarded as a personal individual. Individuals exist in time, and the idea of any being, however conceived, for whom time never passes, who cannot think (since thought involves time), who simultaneously knows every single event in the past, present and future, who is omnipresent and who is totally immutable, stretches the idea of an 'individual' to breaking point and and maybe beyond. It is probably fairer, indeed, to say that this God cannot be known (see chapter 2) – he 'is', but the believer cannot know 'what is'.

If God cannot be known, it must be even more questionable as to whether he can be experienced. Since he is timeless, any experience would have to be mediated, as we can only experience things that exist in time and space. So here again we have the idea of experiencing God in our relationships with others or in events in the world about us. In coming to know others, the believer comes to know God. Those who see God in these terms are not likely to differ materially when defining their religious experiences from those who maintain that God is a reality within the believing community or that talk of God affirms a different way in which life can be lived. The main area of difference would be if supporters of this view were to maintain that God can act in the world (as they normally claim – even though, as we have seen, this is subject to question); they might then point to specific events as being 'acts of God'. However, as so much will depend on the interpretation given to particular events or actions rather than to qualities in the events or actions themselves, this again brings us back to a view which is not dissimilar to the first two we looked at above.

5 Summary

Religious experiences normally occur within faith rather than serving as a foundation for faith. Much will depend on the interpretation brought to particular experiences, and the validation of an experience as 'religious' is likely to be more in terms of the effects it has on the individual who has the experience than on specific qualities within the experience itself. There is no single method of validation, but there are pointers and indicators.

Holders of all four views of God can maintain that they have religious experiences and there will be a large degree of agreement about the areas of experience which can be described as religious. Straightforwardly, those who maintain that God is personal and everlasting do have the option of claiming direct experience of God, although this would tend to be more in the form of an awareness of God rather than anything more direct. Those who consider God to be timeless substance need to recognise that there is almost nothing that they can know of God or what it is to be God and they may, therefore, be more likely to find God within people they meet or in everyday life.

9

What Is an Atheist?

Socrates was accused of being an atheist because, it was alleged, he did not believe in the gods of the Athenian state. In the Roman Emire, Christians were described as atheists because they rejected the Roman gods. Today an atheist is generally regarded as someone who does not believe in any God or gods – often such a position will go hand in hand with MATERIALISM (the belief that, fundamentally, there is only one substance in the universe – matter – and that everything is derived from matter. Thought, beauty, the moral order and similar so-called 'higher' faculties of man can all, therefore, be explained without the need to posit a God or any transcendent spiritual order outside the material universe).

Just as we have seen that there are various possible definitions of God, so there are various possible forms of atheism, depending on the view of God that is being used. The simplest way to illustrate this is by reference to the four conceptions of God set out in chapter 3.

1 God as personal and everlasting

Believers in God as defined by this option maintain that God is a personal being or spirit who exists apart from the universe that he has created but yet is continuously interactive with it. He cares for his creation and, specifically, for each individual human being. Human beings can then enter into a personal relationship with him in prayer, can love him and can, after death, continue the relationship with him that has been commenced in this life. Such a view of God is closest to the surface-level biblical approach, although it can be considered to make God into something like a Superman figure, almost an 'old man with a white beard'.

An atheist, on this view, would simply maintain that there is no such being or spirit as God. It is as if I were to explain to my seven-year-old daughter after she has watched a disturbing film, 'Frankenstein is not real, he does not really exist.' So the atheist might say, 'God is not real, he does not really exist.' He or she might go on to explain why believers have recourse to the idea of God (possibly he might say this was due to psychological need or due to an inadequate examination of beliefs fostered in childhood which have no sound basis). Believer and atheist differ about a matter of fact – whether or not there is a being called 'God'.

This is the form of atheism put forward by Bertrand Russell in *Why I Am Not a Christian* (Allen and Unwin 1957), and others who have become atheists also reject this picture of God. However, they are not alone in doing so; those who maintain that God is timeless substance or a reality to be found within the language of the believing community or that talk of God affirms a different way of living life would also reject this approach to 'God'. Care is required therefore, as if those who believe in this view of God take too firm a stand, they will find themselves calling other committed Christians atheists!

Conversion would involve bringing the atheist to accept a factual claim that he or she had previously rejected. Just as someone might not believe that there were black swans until he could be shown that there were black swans, so the atheist would have to be 'shown' (not, of course, literally but by being brought to accept the truth of the statement) that God does exist as in some sense a personal and everlasting individual who created the world and on whom the world still depends.

2 God as timeless substance

The idea of God as a being – a person or indeed as an individual of any sort in a manner akin to individual things found within the universe – is held by some to be religiously inadequate. God is not, it is maintained, a thing but 'being itself', 'undifferentiated unity', 'the totality of all on who all depend', 'pure actuality' or, perhaps, the 'ground of our being'. Above all, God is 'other than' us. He is infinite and totally transcendent and cannot, therefore, be understood or comprehended by man, who is finite and is located within the universe of space and time. God is literally timeless – he is outside time and space.

As we saw in chapter 2, this approach leads the believer to be very agnostic about God. He or she can know *that* God is without having any idea *what* he is. The believer cannot even know what it means to say that 'God loves us' or that 'God created the world'. These expressions are based on analogy or metaphor, and the language in the Bible about God would also be metaphorical – it can provide helpful and possibly true pictures of God's otherness, but it must not be taken literally nor can it be understood what it means for this language to be true. God is, necessarily, hidden behind mystery and this mystery cannot be uncovered or explained.

The atheist, according to this view, would be someone who rejected this whole idea of God; possibly he or she might maintain that this talk of mystery covered up an illusion and there was no reality behind it to be known. It is one thing to maintain that God is unknowable and 'other', but the believer can nevertheless grope, however inadequately, towards trying to explain to the non-believer what God is. If, however, there is no God towards which the believer is trying to move, then he is mistaken in his quest. It is one thing for the Knights of King Arthur's Round Table to seek the Holy Grail even though they may never find it, it is quite another for someone to say that there is no such thing and the search itself is unimportant.

Here, however, we come to one of the difficulties involved in this approach to God. God is made so transcendent, so far above man, so much 'other-than' man, that it can become open to question as to just what reality is actually being maintained.

It is not too large a step for the outsider to religion to say to the believer in God: 'You can know nothing of this God who you say exists. The most you can say is that "God is", and you admit that you have no idea what he is. You even agree that as we are finite, no theologian's search for God is ever going to be successful. Surely it is rather like the Holy Grail. What is important is the search itself, not that there has to be some 'substance' at the end of the search. You should, therefore, concentrate on how life is lived without indulging in pointless metaphysical speculation.'

This is a persuasive position and it leaves the believer with a dilemma. Either:

(a) He or she has to be rather more specific about just what it is that he or she believes in – and this, in principle, is difficult on this view. Or:

(b) The believer must admit that it is the religious life that is important and defining God is not a major issue for the individual believer.

Once this second option is taken, the believer cannot then criticise those who look on God as an existing reality within the language of religious believers. There is no longer great importance in the unknowable 'something' out there. What is vital is the religious life that the believer lives and the quality of this life is not going to be determined by assent to particular propositions which, in any case, are going to be difficult to define. As we have seen, the particular view of 'God' which is adopted is going to have a decisive influence on what can be said about prayer, miracle, eternal life, evil and similar issues, so if a definition of God does not matter too much, then, on the same basis, a definition of what these other terms mean may also not be regarded as important.

Given that the view of God as timeless substance is most prevalent within the Roman Catholic community, it might seem that the idea of agnosticism about what 'God is' is surprising. Popular wisdom has it that the Roman Catholic Church stands for certainty put out by means of dogmatic statements of belief expressed in propositional terms. This, however, is a false picture. First, there are very few statements of DOGMA (a dogma is a religious truth held to be established by divine revelation and defined by the Church). Even these few statements are expressed in language which needs interpretation. One of the great strengths of the Roman Catholic Church is that it has always recognised the need for the interpretation of theological language – whether this is the language of the Bible or Church pronouncements. Once, therefore, the surface level meaning is seen to be inadequate (as it almost invariably is) there is often a wide spread of opinion as to how theological language is to be interpreted. To take one obvious example – the creed refers to Jesus as being seated 'on the right hand of God'. No one, however, takes this literally – it is a helpful metaphor which needs interpretation. If this is the case with a simple statement, it is not surprising that this is even more the case with more complex issues such as what 'God' is.

3 God as a reality within religious language

According to this approach, God is an existing reality found within the believing community and within religious language. 'God talk' involves terms that the believer has a use for (just as a mathematician has a use for prime numbers). The believer knows what terms like redemption, atonement, the Trinity and Last Judgement mean. He or she knows how these terms should be used and they fulfil a role and purpose in the life he or she leads. There is not, however, any 'being, person or spirit' to which the word 'God' relates. God's reality is to be found within the believing community – for instance, when two or three gather together in his name.

An atheist would be someone who has no use for God-talk, who finds no role for or meaning in religious language. Such a person, if attending a church service, might well find the service meaningless; he or she would probably not be stirred or moved by the singing or the preaching and might consider that the whole of religion rests on a mistake. Wittgenstein said that, when he was asked whether he believed in the Last Judgement, he found that he could not say 'No', because he could not really understand what the believer meant by the expression. He simply did not use this expression; he had no use for it, since he did not operate with this type of picture of the world. Atheist and believer do not, according to this view of God, differ about a factual claim as to the existence of some 'being' or 'substance' called God. Rather they differ because the atheist has no use for religious language while to the believer the religious life and the reality of God found

110

within the believing community is the most important thing in life for him or her.

It is open to question whether it makes sense to talk of an 'atheist' under this definition. Certainly it does make sense if by an atheist we mean someone who has no use for religious language and who finds no beauty or meaning in it. However, such an individual must at least recognise that others do find such a meaning and such a value, and he or she would accept that, for the believer, God is a reality even though he or she has no use for this idea. Conversion, according to this view of God, involves bringing the atheist to see the value and purpose in religious language. It involves the individual coming to see a meaning in the religious life where there was no meaning before. Conversion does not require a change in factual beliefs but rather involves coming to accept an altered view of the value and purpose of religion.

4 Talk of God seen as affirming a possible way in which life can be lived

In chapter 6, Stewart Sutherland's quotation from the play *A Man for All Seasons* was discussed. Thomas More tells the ambitious young man, Rich, that he has misunderstood what life is about. Instead of seeking material success he should instead go and become a teacher. More says: 'If you are a good teacher you will know it, your pupils will know it and God will know it.' Sutherland rejects the idea that 'God' here means some everlasting, personal being or timeless substance existing apart from the universe in a transcendent heaven. He does not consider that such a view is any longer tenable. Rather Thomas More is trying to show the young man that there is a way of living life that cannot be trivialised by the way things turn out, it cannot be undermined by the contingencies to which human life is so often susceptible. A teacher's life has a value in its own right and nothing can take this value away. Talk of 'God', therefore, enshrines the possibility of a different way of living life.

We do not have control over much of our lives. A young man or woman may set out with ambitions in the world, but whether these are fulfilled is not entirely dependent on him or her. Much may depend on health, good luck and other factors. If, therefore, someone seeks their own happiness in the material world which they cannot control they constantly risk being disappointed and let down. Only a good life lived for its own sake and without any hope of a reward can really give peace and meaning to life. No matter what happens, the person who is trying to live a good and virtuous life cannot have this taken away. To be sure, the individual may lose material possessions, he or she may even be persecuted and rejected, but such an individual will remain at peace with themselves knowing that, at the end of the day, nothing can separate him or her from the good path that has been chosen. Such a person, upholders of this view might maintain, was perfectly exemplified by Jesus Christ, who showed how a life of love can be lived which is totally fulfilling even though it may end in an agonising death. Jesus' spirit lives on in his Church and in the lives of believers who try to relate their lives to him.

This view is, frankly, revisionary. It sets out to point a way forward for Christianity into the next century and beyond; unlike the linguistic view above, it does not pretend to be an accurate record of what believers currently believe. An atheist, on this view, would be someone who rejects the possibility of living a good life and who maintains that self-sacrifice, the hard and stony virtuous path or, in the end, martyrdom is foolish and rests on a delusion. If, in the end, the saint who lives a dedicated life of self-denial and commitment to others is deluded, then his whole life rests on a mistake. The religious life simply is not a possible way of living life meaningfully. Someone who maintained this would be an atheist. This is certainly a tenable position but it is, perhaps, one that few would sympathise with. Even a hard-line materialist can admire and respect Mother Teresa or Gandhi. If this is the case, if the religious life can be recognised as having value and meaning, then an individual cannot claim to be an atheist as here defined.

It is important to recognise that if 'God-talk' does indeed represent talk of an alternative way of living life that represents a real possibility for humanity, then many people would accept this and there would be relatively few atheists. If someone was an atheist, conversion would take place when he or she was brought to realise that the religious way of life which had previously been thought to be futile and pointless was, indeed, worthwhile and provided a way for each individual to transcend and thus overcome the limitations of his or her finite existence.

5 Summary

What it means to be an atheist depends directly on what is meant by God. A Christian who believes in one view of God may strongly reject another view and may, therefore, be held to be an atheist by supporters of the alternative approach. If atheism simply means rejecting the idea of the reality of God, then few atheists would be found, as most people would admit that, at the least, God exists as a reality for the religious believer or that God-talk affirms a possible way in which life can be lived.

The challenge presented by British philosophers such as Bertrand Russell or David Hume when they rejected God was direct and clear cut. They were rejecting a particular view of God which they considered to be inadequate or meaningless. Today any similar attack would have to be much more sophisticated and more clearly directed. To say 'I do not believe in God' or even, as Russell did, to write a book entitled *Why I Am Not a Christian* first requires a definition of what God means and secondly demands some definition of what it is to be a Christian – and this could hardly be given without, at least implicitly, involving some view of God's reality.

10

The Resurrection – the Final Question

The Lord is risen indeed. (Luke 24:34)

We preach Christ crucified, a stumbling block to Jews and folly to Greeks, but to those who are called, both Jews and Greeks, Christ the power of God and the wisdom of God. (1 Cor. 1:23–4)

If for this life only we have hoped in Christ, we are of all men most to be pitied. But in fact Christ has been raised from the dead, the first fruits of those who have fallen asleep. (1 Cor. 15:19–20)

At the heart of the faith of the early Church was the claim that Jesus Christ had risen from the dead. He had been crucified, had died and three days later had risen and appeared to many of his followers. The growth of the early Church sprang from the resurrection appearances. Before these took place, Jesus' followers were dejected and forlorn. Their friend and leader, of whom they had such high hopes, was dead and there seemed no future at all. No enterprise was ever so completely at an end as was Christianity on the day after Good Friday.

We come here, therefore, to a major divide between our four conceptions of God and to the major issue on which each individual needs to take a stand. *Those who believe in God as either a reality within the believing community or who maintain that talk of God affirms a possible way in which life can be lived will not believe in the resurrection of Jesus Christ from the dead as an individual with his existing memories.* They can still, however, maintain that Jesus was resurrected. Much depends on what you take the word 'resurrected' to mean.

114

There has been much controversy of late as to whether it should be required of a Christian to believe that Jesus rose from the dead with his physical body (thus leaving an empty tomb) or whether he had a spiritual body. This is an entirely legitimate point for theologians to discuss, but it is a comparatively minor point in comparison with the divide between the four different approaches to God that we have been considering. Whether or not Jesus' body was in the tomb really is not very important. Even to those who maintain that he did rise with a physical body, this body must have undergone changes since he could appear in a locked room. The crucial point is not what type of body Jesus may have had, but whether he survived death as an individual with his existing memories.

The phrase 'as an individual with his existing memories' may seem cumbersome, but it is important. As we saw in chapter 6 memory can be argued to be a necessary condition for identity. In other words if pre-mortem Jesus is to be the same individual as post-mortem Jesus then, at the least, he must retain his memories (as the gospel narratives clearly maintain that he did – he recognised his disciples and was clearly aware of all the events leading up to his crucifixion). This phrase is important as it maintains that Jesus was an individual after he died. Not everyone looks on the resurrection in these terms. Jesus may, instead, be seen to be resurrected in that he lives on in the community of believers. He lives on within the Church that he left behind him and his 'spirit' is to be found wherever believers try to follow the commands he laid down. In a parallel fashion we might talk of an individual 'living on in the memories of those who loved her'. This is the most that believers in God as a reality within the language of the believing community could claim. They can talk of resurrection, but it will not be the resurrection of Jesus as an individual.

This can be looked at in two ways. If the resurrection of Jesus from the dead as an individual is considered to be simply too unlikely or improbable, then Christianity may be held to retain its meaning and value. God can still be held to exist, religious language can still provide valuable insights into the human condition and the believing community can help each individual to live a fulfilled life in which he or she will find personal salvation. If, however, Jesus' resurrection as an individual is affirmed, then the believer can go much further and can claim that God exists as a personal and everlasting individual who is apart from the world he has created or that God exists as timeless substance. Both alternatives, as we have seen, enable much more to be claimed about the meaning of prayer, miracle, eternal life and other issues than would otherwise be the case.

The earliest Christian creed was: 'Jesus is Lord.' Those who hold to any of the four views of God discussed in this book can affirm this statement. They could also maintain that:

Jesus was God;
Jesus was born of Mary and crucified under Pontius Pilate;
Jesus was resurrected;
miracles occur;
prayer is meaningful, valid and important;
the believer can have eternal life;
the believer can have religious experiences.

However, as we have seen, believers in the four different views of 'God' may all mean rather different things by these statements. It is not easy to separate those who hold to different approaches to 'God' merely by looking at their other beliefs. One of the very few areas where this separation is possible is in what is meant by the resurrection.

A series of questions can emphasise the point:

1 Do you believe that Jesus of Nazareth rose from the dead as an individual with his existing memories?
If you answer 'Yes', then this will point you towards a God who is either timeless substance or an everlasting, personal individual. If you answer 'No', this would indicate either that God is a reality so be found within the believing community or that 'God-talk' sets out a possible way in which life can be lived.

2 Do you believe that after his death Jesus went to a heavenly kingdom which takes the form of a perfect society of some type?
You can only answer 'Yes' to this if you answered 'Yes' to

(1) above. If you answer 'Yes' to this question as well, this would probably point you towards a God who is an everlasting, personal individual rather than timeless substance (since a timeless God implies a timeless heaven. If God was timeless, Jesus would have 'entered time' during his incarnation and then moved 'out of time' after his death. Heaven would not be a society, since interaction between individuals is a necessary part of any society and this involves time).

If you answered 'yes' to (1) above and 'no' to this question, this would imply that God was literally timeless and that, after death, the individual could hope to enjoy the timeless beatific vision of God.

3 If you answered 'No' to (1), do you believe that, if there were no religious believers at all, God would still exist as some form of reality?

If you answer 'Yes' to this, this would point towards a view of 'God' as a reality which carries implications about the nature of the universe (i.e. it has 'ontological implications'). The universe is such that a good life can be lived and God-talk sets out this possibility. This would suggest Stewart Sutherland's view of God (the fourth of the options in chapter 3).

If you answered 'No', this would imply that God is a reality within the language of religious believers. If, however, there were no believers, there would be no God.

It is right that Christians should be open to different interpretations of their faith and, fortunately, the ecumenical movement continues to grow – not just in terms of churches moving closer together but also individual church members being more aware of and sympathetic to traditions other than their own. The same can be said of relations between the main world religions. Having said this, however, beliefs and the content of beliefs are important and it may be desirable to set limits to what can and what cannot be counted as 'Christian'.

It is right that believers should think about who or what they are worshipping and what their beliefs mean. Christianity has never been afraid of a genuine search for truth.

Certainly God cannot be comprehended by man, but any religious believer must have some views as to what it means to worship God and how to account for the issues dealt with in the previous chapters. This book has aimed to focus attention on the main problems, and my hope is that the reader will be prompted to take his or her inquiries further. At the least, I would hope that people will realise that some philosophers and theologians may be using Christian language but may mean by this language things that our fathers would not have recognised. This does not necessarily mean that the new interpretations are wrong, but they should at least be understood. It is then up to each individual to affirm or to reject them.

It is a legitimate point of debate as to whether those who uphold the different views of God set out in this book can all be regarded as Christians. The claims they all make are often going to be similarly expressed; however, what is meant by this surface-level language may (as we have seen) differ considerably. It is not always easy to draw dividing lines. Indeed, the whole process of drawing dividing lines is one that many would want to resist. Many may nevertheless hold that if an individual cannot believe in the resurrection of Jesus as an individual with his memories, then he or she cannot claim to be a Christian. If this view is taken, this would mean that the third and fourth views of God we have been discussing cannot be called Christian, even though they may have great depth and intellectual profundity. In this sense, the resurrection of Jesus and what this means may still provide the crucial test of orthodoxy and thus pose the final question.

Reading List

This is not intended as an academic book list, but as suggestions for further reading for non-academics. With this as an aim, it is already too long! Books which I would particularly recommend to any interested reader are marked with an asterisk, but these are no more than personal preferences.

Books dealing with the existence of God and general issues in the philosophy of religion but which, however, do not take seriously the different ideas of God dealt with in this book include:

B. Davies, *An Introduction to the Philosophy of Religion* (Oxford 1982).
* J. C. A. Gaskin, *The Quest for Eternity* (Penguin 1984).
* J. L. Mackie, *The Miracle of Theism* (Oxford UP 1982).
  R. Swinburne, *The Existence of God* (Oxford UP 1979).
  J. Hick, *The Existence of God* (Macmillan 1974).

The different attributes of God are dealt with in:

Anthony Kenny, *The God of the Philosophers* (Oxford UP 1979).
* R. H. Nash, *The Concept of God* (Zondervan 1983).

Books specifically dealing with alternative approaches to God include:

* Don Cupitt, *Taking Leave of God* (SCM 1980).
* Keith Ward, *Holding Fast to God* (SPCK 1982).
* Stewart Sutherland, *God, Jesus and Belief* (Blackwell 1984).
  John Hick, *The Myth of God Incarnate* (SCM 1977).
  Charles Hartshorne, *The Divine Relativity* (Yale UP, New Haven, 1948); standard exposition of 'process' thought.
  Alan Keightley, *Wittgenstein, Grammar and God* (Epworth 1976).
  W. D. Hudson, *Wittgenstein and Religious Belief* (Macmillan 1975).
  W. D. Hudson, *A Philosophical Approach to Religion* (Macmillan 1974).
  Dewi Phillips, *Faith and Philosophic Enquiry* (Routledge 1970).
* E. L. Mascall, *He Who Is* (Longman Green 1962); excellent study by a modern scholar in St Thomas' tradition.

M. F. Wiles, *Faith and the Mystery of God* (SCM 1982).
John Robinson, *Honest to God* (SCM 1963).
John Robinson, *Exploration into God* (Mowbray 1977).
Grace Jantzen, *God's World, God's Body* (DLT 1984); good sections on dualism and timelessness.
Nelson Pike, *God and Timelessness* (Schocken, New York, 1970); somewhat dated now, but still the best single attack on the idea of a timeless God being able to act.
Boethius, *The Consolation of Philosophy*, trans. V. Watts (Penguin 1969).
John Haught, *What Is God?* (Gill & MacMillan 1986); draws heavily on Tillich and is a good statement of his approach to God.
Paul Tillich, *The Shaking of the Foundations* (SCM 1949).
Anthony Kenny's 'Divine Foreknowledge and Human Freedom' (in *Aquinas: A Selection of Critical Essays*, ed. A. Kenny. Doubleday, New York, 1969) and Paul Helm's 'Timelessness and Foreknowledge' (*Mind 84*, 1975) are worthwhile articles on the problems of timelessness.

Books on Aquinas form an industry in themselves. One of the best general introductions is *F. Copleston's *Aquinas* (Search Press 1976), and this has a helpful bibliography. After reading this, there is much to be said for browsing through the *Summa Theologiae* itself. It is an enormous work, first sight of it will be daunting and a superficial reading can be misleading; nevertheless it may make a better starting point than by going to commentators, particularly as the index is good.

Books with sections on miracles include:
* Stewart Sutherland, *Atheism and the Rejection of God* (Blackwell 1977).
John Gaskin, *The Quest for Eternity* (Penguin 1984).
John Mackie, *The Miracle of Theism* (Oxford UP 1982).
A. Flew and A. MacIntyre, *New Essays in Philosophical Theology* (SCM 1972).
* David Hume, *Enquiries Concerning the Human Understanding and Concerning the Principles of Morals*, ed. Selby-Bigge (Oxford UP 1902).

Books relating to prayer include:
C. S. Lewis, *Letters to Malcolm* (Fontana 1966).
* Vincent Brummer, *What Are We Doing when We Pray?* (SPCK 1984).
* Dewi Phillips, *The Concept of Prayer* (Routledge 1968).
P. Baelz, *Does God Answer Prayer?* (DLT 1982).

Books relating to eternal life include:
* Dewi Phillips, *Death and Immortality* (Macmillan 1970).
  John Donnelly, *Language, Metaphysics and Death* (Fordham UP 1978); series of articles by different philosophers covering diverse related topics.
  John Hick, *Death and Eternal Life* (Collins 1976).
  Karl Rahner, *The Theology of Death* (Nelson 1961).
  Gilbert Ryle, *The Concept of Mind* (Penguin 1970); classic argument against the dualist position.

Books dealing with the problem of evil are many and various. They include:
  Austin Farrer, *Love Almighty and Ills Unlimited* (Fontana 1966).
* Alvin Plantinga, *God, Freedom and Evil* (Allen & Unwin 1975).
* Peter Geach, *Providence and Evil* (Cambridge UP 1971).
  M. B. Ahern, *The Problem of Evil* (Routledge 1971).
  John Hick, *Evil and the God of Love* (Fontana 1968).

Bertrand Russell's *Why I Am Not a Christian* (Allen & Unwin 1957) is worthwhile as a rejection of the traditional idea of God. Plato's *The Last Days of Socrates* (Penguin 1976) is a good way of entering Plato's whole authorship.

Index